James Albert Green

The Dream of Ellen N

James Albert Green

The Dream of Ellen N

ISBN/EAN: 9783337345389

Printed in Europe, USA, Canada, Australia, Japan

Cover: Foto ©Thomas Meinert / pixelio.de

More available books at **www.hansebooks.com**

THE
DREAM OF "ELLEN N"

AN ILLUSTRATED

DESCRIPTIVE AND HISTORIC NARRATIVE

OF

SOUTHERN TRAVELS.

ISSUED UNDER THE AUSPICES OF THE

LOUISVILLE AND NASHVILLE RAILROAD PASSENGER DEPARTMENT,

LOUISVILLE, KY.

PUBLISHED BY
JOHN P. C. MULLEN,
CINCINNATI, U.S.A.

Entered according to Act of Congress in the Year 1880, by

JOHN F. C. MULLEN,

In the Office of the Librarian of Congress, at Washington

All Rights Reserved.

PUBLISHER'S NOTICE.

In presenting this book to the public the publisher desires to say a few words. He wishes to call attention to its many excellencies, and the original ideas in its style, "get-up" and contents. As can be seen, the publication of a volume as complete as "THE DREAM OF ELLEN N." involves an immense amount of labor. Yet labor, pains or expense have not been spared to make it a success, and the publisher believes that it will be accorded without question the first place among railroad books of its kind. Well-known and skillful artists have been employed to make the illustrations, and the work in this respect is as fine as anything that has ever been seen in the country. No finer or more artistic engravings will be found in the "Century" or the "Harper's," which are famous the world over for the beauty and truthfulness of their illustrations. The names of the artists, which are given elsewhere, will be recognized at once, while of course their pictures speak for them. And not only have the artists been men of rare ability, but they have been seconded in their work by the engravers, better than whom there are none in America.

The literary features of the volume are not to be forgotten. It is no mere guide-book, but a most readable history of the Louisville and Nashville Railroad and its many branches. The traveler who reads it has presented to him a truthful picture of the ground he is passing over, of the cities he visits, and of the people and their various pursuits. And on the line of the L. & N. are many famous and historic places, which are fully described, and the tourist is told in an interesting way of what is to be seen and the way to see it. Special attention has been paid to schools, colleges and educational institutions, which are situated in great numbers along the line of the road, and the many watering places and "resorts" are mentioned at length.

But "THE DREAM OF ELLEN N." speaks for itself. It is like good wine, in that it needs no bush, and words of introduction are unnecessary. In conclusion, however, the publisher would like to call the attention of railroad corporations to the benefits resulting to themselves from such publications, and to state that he has special facilities for publishing books of this kind. He is ready to do the work on short notice, and is at all times prepared to furnish estimates and designs. He has an organized corps of artists and engravers, whose experience in this particular line is most valuable, while his mechanical facilities for making a handsome volume typographically can not be excelled.

Railroads thinking of issuing such a publication are respectfully asked to communicate with

JOHN F. C. MULLEN, PUBLISHER.

ADDRESS
JOHN F. C. MULLEN,
aville & Nashville Ticket Office,
CINCINNATI, OHIO

LIST OF ILLUSTRATIONS.

SUBJECT	ARTISTS.	ENGRAVERS.
Louisville & Nashville Passenger Station.	ROBERT MCFEE.	McFee & Co.
Along the Short Line.	T. C. LINDSAY.	McFee & Co.
Bellewood Seminary.	PAUL JONES.	McFee & Co.
Crab Orchard.	PAUL JONES.	McFee & Co.
Hamilton Female College.	ALBERT E. EVANS.	McFee & Co.
Agricultural and Mechanical College.	ALBERT E. EVANS.	McFee & Co.
Home School for Young Ladies.	V. NOWOTNY.	McFee & Co.
Bethel College.	ALBERT E. EVANS.	M. B. Hall.
Dunbar Cave.	PAUL JONES.	McFee & Co.
Evergreen Lodge.	PAUL JONES.	McFee & Co.
Clarksville Tobacco Exchange.	M. B. HALL.	M. B. Hall
Louisville Hotel.	ALBERT E. EVANS.	McFee & Co.
The Home of "Ellen N."	PAUL JONES.	McFee & Co.
Mammoth Cave.	PAUL JONES.	McFee & Co.
McIlbrough's Hill	T. C. LINDSAY.	McFee & Co.
Ogden College.	ALBERT E. EVANS.	McFee & Co.
Southern Normal School and Business College.	ALBERT E. EVANS.	McFee & Co.
Henderson Bridge.	V. NOWOTNY.	McFee & Co.
W. E. Ward's Seminary for Young Ladies.	V. NOWOTNY.	McFee & Co.
Nashville.	ALBERT E. EVANS.	McFee & Co.
Nashville by Moonlight.	ALBERT E. EVANS.	McFee & Co.
Vanderbilt University.	ROBERT MCFEE.	McFee & Co.
Sand Mountain.	T. C. LINDSAY.	McFee & Co.
First National Bank of Birmingham.	ROBERT MCFEE.	McFee & Co.
The Sunny South.	T. C. LINDSAY.	McFee & Co.
Pensacola Bay.	T. C. LINDSAY.	L. B. Folger.
The Home of Jefferson Davis.	C. A. FRIES.	McFee & Co.
Lagoons by Moonlight.	T. C. LINDSAY.	McFee & Co.
New Orleans.	C. A. FRIES.	McFee & Co.
Cover.	H. L. BRIDWELL.	M. B. Hall.
Cover	PAUL JONES	M. B. Hall.

"Well, Bea."
"Well, brother mine."
"We've started."

AND as I spoke the Pullman gently glided forward and we had started on our trip to the "sunny southland." I am one of those Americans who believe that this country is the greatest and grandest that the sun shines upon, and it is a part of my religion to see it and know it before going abroad. I believe that there are just as many tours, as they call them, in America as there are in Europe, and that they are vastly more profitable to the tourist, for here he is in the land of the living and not wandering among the dusty relics of departed greatness and the mummies of long dead and buried enterprise as on the other side of the water. And so when the opportunity came during the Christmas holidays to take a trip, my sister and myself packed up our traps and started for a ramble over the South on the L. & N., or "Ellen N," as we affectionately called the road from the very beginning of our travels. Of course there was a great deal of preliminary planning and much studying of maps before our arrangements were complete. In order to make the way easier for other travelers I have jotted down our experiences in this book. Cincinnati was our starting point, and in a moment or two we were rumbling over the massive iron bridge that spans the Ohio, and the city, with its teeming thousands, and miles and miles of noble buildings, was left behind. Cincinnatians see this bridge so much that they seldom stop to think what a wonderful structure it is, yet it is built to defy time. Its mighty stone piers and iron trusses not only bear the traffic of a great railroad, but over its footways there flow two unceasing streams of vehicles and people between Cincinnati and its fair young sister city Newport. But we are fairly across the Ohio and in the South, and not only in the South but in Kentucky, that blissful region of fair maidens and gallant men. And Newport has more than its proportion of beautiful girls and brave men, and it is noted for its blue blooded families and generous hospitality as much as the other Newport is famous for its summer cottages and gorgeous display. Newport, however, is very familiar to every Cincinnatian visits there, and Bea simply remarks on the extreme quiet of the place in contrast to the bustle across the river.

"Look," she cried, "we're running right in the middle of the street, just as though we were in a carriage." And this is true, for the L. & N. goes directly through the town in a masterful kind of way, not skirting it and stealing through the slums and back yards as is often the case in railroad approaches.

There is only a moment's stop at Newport, and then the train starts on its picturesque run to Louisville over the Short line. Six miles out is "Latonia" station, and the track and great airy buildings of the Latonia Race Course are within a stone's throw. Here it is that the famous Kentucky thoroughbred "Leonatus" made such a wonderful record, while nearly all of the great horses of the country have shown their paces as they sped round and round the course. The races are great events and they are not only attended by the wealth and beauty of the three cities of Cincinnati, Covington and Newport, but half of Kentucky gathers to see them, and the grand stand is a brilliant sight on a field-day. Talk about beautiful women! They are there by the hundreds and they are not only fair of face, they are well built, graceful, and as the Kentuckian horse fancier said bestowing praise with the most expressive smile of which he was capable, "they are more symmetrical than a thoroughbred."

The track at Latonia has a most excellent reputation among sportsmen and it is considered one of the finest in the country. The first race meeting took place in June, 1883, and there was a larger continuous attendance, heavier purses given away, and a greater number of thoroughbreds gathered together than was ever before known in the South or West, and this auspicious beginning has been of a piece with its succeeding history. Truthfully and beautifully has it been written:

"Latonia—sweet sounding in name,
Paradise of horsemen."

Latonia has done a great deal, and is doing a great deal, to encourage the breeding of fine horses. It offers that practical encouragement in the shape of financial rewards to the horseman who succeeds in developing the fleetest-footed steeds, and it might be remarked that Kentucky has ever been noted for its horseflesh. The early Virginians, who settled the State, were lovers of racing, and they brought their horses with them. In course of time the breed was improved by the importation of animals from Pennsylvania, and the settlers began to discover that the water and soil of Kentucky brought out the best points of horses, and that in two or three generations of horses the swift became swifter and the clean-footed, long-necked, slim-built, became cleaner footed, longer necked and slimmer built. In fact they awoke to the fact that "blue grass" and lime water were making such horses as the world has never seen.

And Kentucky is one of the great horse growing and horse using States of the Union. When the war broke out the most daring bands of horsemen came from there. It was there that Morgan organized his company of wild rangers, and it was Kentucky horses that tirelessly carried them over field and flood on their desperate expeditions. His men were Kentuckians trained to the saddle from youth, and their free and easy style of performing cavalry evolutions would have astonished a prime German or English officer. But they knew how to manage their horses and they did more execution in a shorter space of time during the war than did any other body of men of the same size. At one time their mere approach threw the whole of the great city of Cincinnati into turmoil, while by one fierce rally they spread terror and dismay throughout Southern Illinois, Indiana and Ohio.

But I am not writing war reminiscences. That must be left to the Century Magazine. I simply started to say something about Kentucky horses and strayed a little from the subject. The rank and file of these horses still, however, have occasionally a chance to distinguish themselves in military services, for the English government buys hundreds of them annually for the army. At the time of the Arabi Bey rebellion in Egypt, the English also bought all the Kentucky mules in the Cincinnati market for use in the war. So it can be seen that the breeding of horses has been turned to great practical account. Thousands of dollars are invested in some of the blue grass stock farms and they are managed with the same precision and system as a mercantile business.

While we are thus entering and passing through the "dark and bloody ground," as it was called in the old Indian days, a glance at its varied history may be interesting. A hundred years ago and more, all this region was known as Transylvania, and it was free from settlers of any kind. The red men had no permanent villages here but simply roamed through the country on hunting expeditions. Occasionally white hunters came here, too, and they brought back reports of the beauty and fertility of the region. Among these early comers was Dr. Thomas Walker, a Virginian, who in 1750 journeyed as far as where Lexington now stands, and his diary still exists. As Shaler, in his history of Kentucky, says: "He seems to have been a remarkably intelligent explorer, for he noticed the easternmost outcrop of the Appalachian coal field, which so far is probably the first mention of any fact of geological nature concerning any part of the Virginian mountains." These early wanderers were all enthusiastic, and in 1774—June 10 is the exact date—the first deliberate attempt was made to form a permanent settlement. James Harrod, with forty companions sailed down the Ohio to a point near Louisville, and then striking inland they penetrated to Central Kentucky, where they founded what is now the flourishing and historic town of Harrodsburg. Then came Boone and the brave pioneers who followed where he led. In 1775 a frontier congress was held at Boone's Station and the following laws were passed: an act to establish courts of judicature and establish practice therein; an act for regulating the militia; an act for the punishment of criminals; an act to prevent profane swearing and Sabbath breaking; an act for writs of attachment; an act for ascertaining clerks and sheriffs' fees; an act for to preserve the range (that is, the right of public pasture); an act for preserving the breed of horses, and a game act.

The reader can see that even in that remote day the horse was dear to the Kentucky heart. But the fact that this woodland congress was held, and that these laws were passed, is all important in showing the character of the men who had thus ventured into the wilderness to make homes for themselves and to carve out a State.

ALONG THE SHORT-LINE—KENTUCKY BEACH FOREST

It would be useless to repeat the story of the trials and adventures of these bold settlers. It is a bloody narrative, full of border heroism, of midnight attack and murderous reprisal, of snake-like cunning watched by unceasing watchfulness and brave endurance, of savage torture and death, and of final triumph for the whites. After the Revolutionary war the Indians were driven westward and northward and the pioneers were left practically undisturbed. However, at the very beginning of the Revolutionary struggle, in 1776, the name of Transylvania was dropped and Kentucky County was officially separated from Fincastle County, Virginia, Harrodsburg being named as the seat of government. The growth of the territory was rapid, and in 1792 it was admitted into the Union. Says Shaler: "From the settlement of Harrodsburg in 1774, to the admission of Kentucky into the Union, was seventeen years. In these crowded years, full of incessant battle with the wilderness and its tenants, a struggle in which thousands of brave men fell, a State had been created. For nearly one-half the time during which this great work was a-doing, the parent colony of Virginia was engaged in a war that drained her energies to utter exhaustion.

"There is no similar spectacle in history that is so curious as this swarming of men into the wilderness during the time when their mother country was engaged in a life and death struggle. We can only explain it through the intense land-hunger which marks the Saxon people. The thirst for land which we find so strongly developed in the Elizabethian English, seems to have been transmitted to Virginia in an intenser form. Knowing that free lands were to be won by giving life for it, the Virginia and North Carolina people were driven to desert their comfortable dwelling places in the colonies for the battle in the West. There is no other case where this land-winning motive is so clearly seen as here. All our other western immigration has been fostered by the protection of the government. These people could look to no protection but what they gave themselves."

The history of Kentucky until the Civil War is a narrative of uninterrupted prosperity and steady growth. It was marked by the brilliant episode of the Mexican war, in which Kentucky soldiers particularly distinguished themselves. Gen. Zachary Taylor was a Kentuckian, and the glorious victory at Buena Vista was won almost entirely by the regiments from his native State. Of course the history of the Commonwealth in the late "unpleasantness" is well known. At first Kentucky resolved to remain neutral and keep invaders from her soil. But this could not be and the policy of neutrality was abandoned. The State stuck by the Union, yet more than 30,000 of her brave sons marched away to fight for the Confederacy. A still greater number fought under the old flag, but in '65 their battles were over and they returned to their homes to live together in the delights of restored peace, confidence and well being. There was no fighting of the war over again when the Northern and Southern veterans came home. Neighbors again became brothers and joined in the common cause of making the land blossom as the rose, and restoring the prosperity which reigned before the war.

All passenger trains on the "Short-line" make splendid time, and the rapid flight across a corner of Kentucky is hugely enjoyable. For four or five miles the road runs near the banks of the yellow and turbulent Licking, that fierce little river which occasionally rises in its might and pours its swollen waters against the craft lying at the Cincinnati levee, working untold damage and destruction. But just now its muddy current looks peaceful enough, and as we rattle across it and plunge into the Kentucky hills we look back and catch our last glimpse of the great smoke-cloud—that banner of industry—which forever hangs above the "Queen City."

"That is the last of Cincinnati for many a long day," I observe, and then a sudden turn hides the smoky cloud.

The "Short-line" cuts directly across the State, making the shortest possible route between Cincinnati and Louisville. Much of the scenery along the road is very fine. Now the train is curving around a hill whose sides are covered with long rows of tobacco plants, while a noble stretch of valley, rich with woodland and meadow, is to be seen from the car window; then it is rumbling over some high embankment or whizzing through a tunnel. Many are the glimpses of beautiful scenery along the road, and the traveler who passes over it in the spring time finds it a veritable path of flowers. All the hillsides are radiant with bloom while the trees are dressed in colors that might make the gorgeous bird of Paradise ruffle his feathers in envy. It was at this season that our artist sketched the beautiful and restful scene. "Along the Short-line," which is one of the handsomest engravings ever made in America. There are some very pretty towns along the line which are centers of local trade and depots of agricultural products.

But the ride is of truth "short" and almost before we were aware, we were approaching Louisville. After leaving La Grange, which is only twenty-seven miles from Louisville, and which is a flourishing place, suburban houses began to make their appearance. All this stretch of country is destined to grow, and eventually it will be one long, continuous suburb from Louisville. As the city becomes more and more a manufacturing center, the desirability of living beyond the noise and smoke will increase, and as the suburbs follow the railroads it is highly probable that soon this region will be well built up. All the indications point that way, and year by year the number of suburban residents grows greater. It is very likely that some day this country along the "Short-line" will be as popular as that along the roads running out of Cincinnati. In that great and unexpressibly dirty city the people have found it necessary to seek the country with its freshness and purity, and as a consequence the suburbs of Cincinnati are larger than any others in America. And people in Louisville are gradually moving out into the "open" in the same way. This region offers great advantages to the city resident. In the first place it is easily accessible, and then it is high and free from malarial influences. In summer it is always cooler than in the city, as the breeze has a chance to make itself felt. Of course it is a wonderfully good place to bring up a family of boys, uniting, as it does, all the wholesome associations of country life with the advantages of the city, while at the same time being beyond its harmful tendencies. Pewee Valley is one of the prettiest of the suburbs, and it is the home of many Louisville business men. Kentucky College is located here, and as a college town it has additional interest in the eyes of the tourist ; then comes Anchorage which is known everywhere through the State, as the Insane Asylum is situated here. The institution can be seen from the car windows, and Bea and I hardly knew which to admire most, the tasteful building or the beautifully kept grounds.

Anchorage is a suburb of Louisville and it is one of the loveliest and best known in the South. Originally it was called by the unromantic and prosaic name of Hobb's Station, being called for a former President of the Louisville & Lexington R. R. Co. Its picturesque and attractive surroundings give it a peculiarly home-like appearance; and some years since a member of Mr. Hobbs' family suggested a change of name, and that it be called Anchorage, as in description of its restful and peaceful surroundings. The idea was approved, and the station became known under its present name. Many elegant, handsome homes have been erected here, and it has been for many years a great educational center. Dr. H. B. McCown, a distinguished scholar, founded Forest Home Academy, a mile east of the station, and in twenty years since Dr. Hill located Bellewood Seminary near the station. Anchorage is also the home of Bellewood Female Seminary, one of the best known educational centers in the South and West. It is splendidly

BELLEWOOD SEMINARY.

located in a grove of magnificent shade trees and all its environments are unsurpassed for natural beauty and healthfulness. It is several hundred feet above the level of Louisville and malaria is unknown. In the immediate vicinity are many fine residences, the homes of wealthy people doing business in the city, and who come here to escape its turmoil and restlessness in the pure air and quietude of the country. And the purely educational features of the institution are all that could be wished. The course of study is thorough and complete, while the young ladies are also taught what are known as the "accomplishments," that is music, drawing, and the polite arts. Prof. R. C. Morrison is the Principal, Miss Pauline Brock is the lady Principal, Rev. E. W. Bedinger is Chaplain, and Col. Bennet A. Young, of Louisville, is Regent.

After leaving Anchorage came another and lesser suburb, and a few minutes more than four hours after starting, we rolled past the houses and factories which indicated a great city, and the porter, gathering up the ladies' wraps, cried out "Louisville." Bea and I had left Cincinnati at 7:35 A. M. and we were in Louisville at 12:20 P. M. Had we been going directly through we would have taken the Pullman, but as we intended to stop over at Louisville we rode in the chair car, seats in which are furnished the patrons of the road without extra charge. Tourists who are going through direct, however, can take a Pullman Buffet Sleeper at Cincinnati and go without change to New Orleans; or, they can take it at Louisville and go without change to Pensacola and Jacksonville in Florida.

CONNECTIONS AT LOUISVILLE

Knoxville Line

Seldom it is that one finds a prettier or more varied stretch of road than the Knoxville branch of the L. & N. It runs from Lebanon Junction, on the main line, through some of the most picturesque parts of Kentucky, and passes through some of the wildest and most beautiful scenery in Tennessee, to that enterprising and ever-increasing city, Knoxville. The distance from Louisville to Knoxville is two hundred and sixty-one miles, not at all an insignificant jaunt. In England a road of this extent would be called a great through trunk line; but here, in spite of its miles and miles of gleaming steel, it is only a branch.

The first large town on the road, after leaving the junction, is Lebanon, with about three thousand inhabitants. It is a flourishing place, well supplied with churches, schools and manufactories; and, being in the center of a rich farming country, it boasts an extensive trade.

Beyond Lebanon the traveler notices those peculiarly sharp, conical hills called "knobs" by the natives. Their summits against the horizon look like the teeth of some gigantic saw, or like the waves of the ocean in a choppy sea.

At Danville Junction, four miles south of Danville, the track is crossed by the Cincinnati Southern Railroad. There is but little need to speak of Danville, that ancient place of great renown, from whose schools have gone so many of the distinguished men of the State, and among whose residents are the foremost families of Kentucky. It is a town where wealth, education, culture and trade have long centered, and it is a lovely place beside. Near Danville Junction are the famous Alum Springs of Kentucky, whose curative powers have long been well known. Annually they are visited by hundreds, who either seek bodily relief, or, in the peace and quiet of the place, recruit their wasted strength.

Stanford, one hundred and four miles from Louisville, is a town which is steadily growing, and is now of considerable importance. All around lies one of the finest grazing countries in the world—a perfect sea of emerald fields—whose possibilities have as yet hardly been attempted.

And now the road begins to enter the mountainous region of Southeastern Kentucky, and the track winds around steep hills and through rocky cuts, like a vast metallic serpent. At Richmond Junction passengers change cars for Richmond, which lies but thirty-four miles to the north.

Crab Orchard

What Saratoga is to New York, the White Sulphur Springs to Virginia, that is what Crab Orchard to Kentucky. And not to Kentucky alone; for the fame of the Crab Orchard Springs, and the beauty and attractiveness of their surroundings, every year brings hundreds of visitors from the neighboring States. Nowhere in the Union is there a more charmingly lovely spot than here; while the soft and lazy summer climate is a balm to the weary body and tired mind. The springs are about a mile distant from the little town on the railroad, in a valley which is so extensive, that, were it not for the spurs and foot-hills running into it, it might be taken for a plain. Far away can be seen the blue hills, misty by reason of distance; and all around is a country which is a living harmony in color.

Here it is that, regularly as the summer comes, that the beauty and bravery of the country gather. And the merry-makings that absorb old and young, the moonlight rambles, the long daylight walks, the pleasant drives, the joyous picnics, the gay dances, the innocent love-making—who can describe them? You that have had the exquisite pleasure of spending a season at Crab Orchard know of its delights; and know that it would be vain for me to attempt to tell of its numberless pleasures and attractions. Those that come here, brain-worn and wearied by the busy and pressing world, find the very atmosphere of the place contagious; and they give themselves up wholly and unreservedly to the enjoyment of the passing hour. As the poet says, they "leave care and care behind." And who could have a care at Crab Orchard? Care is banished, and joy and mirth rule supreme.

Crab Orchard

This excellent engraving gives the stranger some faint idea of the beauties of the place and its romantic surroundings. The tree lined, shady walks, "leafy arcades," as they have been called, are wonderfully inviting, while the less pretentious paths, winding down to the various springs, seem to repeat to the strolling couples that "two is company, three is a crowd." At least they have been made with such designing skill that often they are only wide enough for two, and this is the reason that the young people pair off so naturally; and, speaking of pairing off, they do say that there are more matches made during the season at Crab Orchard than in all the rest of Kentucky put together. But this is probably only a base rumor, gotten up to frighten timid mammas and suspicious papas. Nevertheless, if it is true that matches are made in heaven, then this delightful resort can lay claim to being an earthly paradise that invalids, beneath, wave pretty closely. But the Springs are **not only** famous as a pleasure resort; they **are** almost better known for their health-giving qualities. Those **who are** troubled with their digestion—that awful bugbear of modern America, and of which **our** forefathers **were** more or less ignorant—find almost immediate relief, while others, afflicted in different ways, **are** signally benefited. These Springs are so numerous and so varied in character that **the invalid** is indeed difficult to please who can not be suited. The Epsom Spring is even better than the **famous** fountain in England, from which it takes its **name**. Then there are Chalybeate Springs of various strength, combined with sulphur, while **the** purity **of the** mountain air **is an** able auxiliary to the waters. **The** hotels are excellent, the company **is** at all times **of the** best, and the man or woman **who has ever** visited Crab Orchard **and not** been **hugely** pleased is unknown.

We furnish an analysis of the principal mineral waters of Crab Orchard Springs, taken from the second report of the Geological Survey in Kentucky, by David Dale Owen. Composition on the basis of one thousand grains.

THE BROWN SPRING.

Carbonate of Iron,		0.028	
	Maganese,	.015	Held in solution in the water by Carbonic Acid
	Lime,	.117	
	Magnesia,	.020	
Sulphate of	"	.112	
	" Lime,	.015	
	" Potash,	.028	
Chloride of Sodium,		.018	
Silicia,		.046	
Moisture and **loss**,		.053—0.442 grains.	

AMERICAN EPSOM SPRING,

FROM WHICH THE SALTS ARE MADE.

Carbonate of Lime,		0.506	Held in solution by Carbonic Acid.
" Magnesia,		.375	
" Iron, a trace			
Sulphate of Magnesia,		2.989	
" Lime,		1.566	
" Potash,		.298	
" Soda,		.398	
" **Sodium**		1.000	
Silicia,		.021—7.153 grains.	
	Bromine a trace.		

THE FIELD SPRING.

Carbonate of Iron and Maganese, 0.015			
" Lime,		.171	Held in solution by Carbonic Acid.
" Magnesia,		.131	
Sulphate of	"	.062	
" " Soda,		.024	
" " Potash,		.022	
Chloride of Sodium,		.008	
Silicia,		.041—0.446 grains.	

The free **Carbonic Acid** present was not estimated.

HOWARD SULPHUR WELL.

Carbonate of Magnesia,		0.065	Held in solution by Carbonic Acid.
" Lime,		.013	
Sulphate of Magnesia,		.012	
" Potash,		.008	
Alumina and trace of Phosphate,		.002	
Chloride of Sodium,		.017	
Silicia,		.022	
Moisture and loss,		.025—0.164 grains.	

THE GROVE SPRING.

Carbonate of Iron,		0.021	
" Maganese,		.005	Held in solution in the water by Carbonic Acid.
" Lime,		.195	
" Magnesia,		.041	
Sulphate of	"	.056	
" Potash,		.013	
Chloride of Sodium,		.013	
Silicia,		.040—0.384 grains.	

The waters of which **the foregoing exhibit shows the** medicinal ingredients, are considered remedial in "Bright's Disease," affections **of the bladder, skin, diseases** of the bowels, neuralgia, scrofula, convalescence from typhoid **and malarial fevers, female diseases, general** debility, etc., under medical advice by the resident physician.

At Broadhead the hills and the mountains really begin to show themselves in something like grand forms, as the **train winds in and out** of deep passes, and the eye confronted by high cliffs, glances occassionally, up deep, **rocky glens, fringed** or almost curtained by **the** thickets of cedar and laurel, and beneath these are discerned brawling and foaming torrents, dashing along over pebbly and stony beds, as they seek their way to the larger streams below. From the edges of the great solid walls of rock, two on either side, which border the track, and above, we come upon small but beautiful **cascades** of crystal water, tumbling down **mossy fronts of cliffs,** each one of these a picture, which, could it be faithfully given, would be a **welcome contribution** to the wealth **of** fine landscapes for which our **country is** already noted.

Livingston, one **hundred and forty miles from Louisville,** is a **place of great promise. Coal** lies in all the hills around, **and iron abounds. The coal is being mined** quite **extensively. The** timber of the vicinity is of **the** best, and as yet the ax of the woodman has not shorn **the hills of their** native beauty. The town lies **at** the meeting place **of the Roundstone Creek and Rockcastle River, which** is crossed by a fine iron bridge.

All the country through **which the road now passes is filled with coal and iron. London,** one hundred and **fifty-seven miles,** will probably be before long **a great mining center. This is** the place where tourists take way for "Rockcastle Springs," eighteen miles distant, and which are delightfully situated in a pleasing country.

Williamsburg is the last large town in Kentucky. After leaving it the road traverses a broken and ever-picturesque country, which is filled with surprises and delights for the eye of the traveler. The valleys **are exceedingly rich, and all kinds of crops** flourish.

Knoxville, the metropolis of Eastern Tennessee, speaks for itself. It is a trim, busy city, filled with vim and enterprise. Here are the East Tennessee, Virginia & Georgia, and the Knoxville & Charleston railroads, which, in connection with the L. & N., give the town excellent railroad connections. It would be idle to say that Knoxville is bound to be an important place. Geographically it is a center, and man has done his part to further its development. It has many factories, and its trade is large. But these are facts which are so well known that to repeat them is almost like saying that New Castle is well supplied with coals. One of the famous products are the beautifully variegated Tennessee marbles, which have been used to such good purpose in the Capitol at Washington, and the New York Capitol at Albany, not to speak of scores of other magnificent public and private buildings. The location of the city is rarely lovely. All around it rise hills, and the diversity of vale and upland is charmingly picturesque.

HAMILTON FEMALE COLLEGE,
LEXINGTON, KY.

Walking up Broadway in Lexington, the most conspicuous building which catches the eye is the Hamilton Female College, which is one of the model educational institutions for young ladies in the country. It is attended by students from all over the land, but more especially from the South, and the work that is done is really excellent. The Faculty, numbering thirteen, is made up of skilled and long-experienced instructors, who enter with a warm sympathy into the aims and aspirations of the pupils. It is this that makes a home-like atmosphere pervade the college, and takes away that hard, dry officialism which too often renders school uninviting. The site of the college is magnificent, overlooking, as it does, all of Lexington; and no pains have been spared to make the grounds attractive. The structure itself is thoroughly modern with every comfort and convenience that is known to the architect or house furnisher.

Cumberland and Ohio Line

This road runs from Lebanon, Kentucky, on the Knoxville line, to Greensburg, about thirty-one miles in a southerly direction. It passes through an excellent agricultural country. Campbellsville, nineteen miles from the starting place, is a pretentious and thriving town. Greensburg is a lovely rural community. It has no factories, but does a large business in the products of the locality.

Bardstown Line

Twenty-two miles south of Louisville, on the main line of the L. & N., is Bardstown Junction, and the town of that name is seventeen miles to the southwest. Three miles out on the branch is Clermont, where is situated one of the finest quarries of stratified limestone in the world. The stone is very easily quarried and readily worked when first removed; but it hardens by exposure. Much of the stone used in the building of the bridge across the Ohio at Louisville came from here, and it is in constant demand. The quarries are owned by the railroad company. At Nazareth is a flourishing Catholic female seminary, and a very imposing collection of buildings. Bardstown is a place of about two thousand five hundred inhabitants. It is substantially built, is the local metropolis, and is quite an educational center.

Bloomfield Line

Bloomfield is an active, aggressive little city, forty-five miles south of Anchorage, on the L. & N Short Line, where the cars are taken to reach it. Shelbyville, nineteen miles, is the principal and largest town on the road. It does a commercial and manufacturing business, and is well furnished with educational institutions. It is in fact one of the towns which is noted throughout Kentucky for push and energy.

Glasgow Line

Glasgow is ten miles west of Glasgow Junction, ninety miles south of Louisville, on the main line of the L. & N. The road runs through a rather hilly country, though it is extremely fertile. Glasgow is a thrifty, solidly-built town, which covers a great deal of ground—all of the inhabitants being believers in the divine right of having just as large yards as may suit their fancy. It is a great shipping point, and the people for fifty miles around regard it as a center. Not far distant are a number of petroleum wells, whose product is about five hundred barrels per month. Glasgow is well supplied with all that ministers to the needs of modern and higher civilization, and it has an expanding future.

Lexington Line

This is a very important and much-traveled road, running from Vadens, on the Short Line, through the State capital, Frankfort, to Lexington, which is situated in the very heart of the world-famous blue grass country. The distance from Louisville is ninety-four miles. Frankfort is a trim little city, which is thronged with statesmen and visitors during the sessions of the legislature, while the State offices always make it a center of political interest. Among the most noted of the public institutions is the penitentiary, which has gained a national reputation during Gov. Blackburn's administration. It is almost superfluous to say aught about Lexington, the second capital of Kentucky, the family home of Henry Clay, and the city where the aristocracy of the State gather annually at the races. It is the capital of the blue grass country, and is famed alike for beautiful women and fast horses. It is no discredit to mention them both in the same breath, for the blue grass horses beat the world, and are second in a Kentuckian's affections only to the ladies of his native State.

Then, too, Lexington is a great educational center. The Agricultural and Mechanical College of Kentucky is situated here. It is a State institution and has an ample endowment, which promises much for the future. Its buildings are located in what was once the City Park, a noble stretch of land containing fifty-two acres, which was given by Lexington to the State. The site is elevated and commands a good view of the city and surrounding country. A new college has been erected, containing commodious chapel, society rooms, lecture and recitation rooms sufficient for the accommodation of six hundred students. A large and well-ventilated dormitory has also been built, with rooms for ninety students, for the use of the appointees sent by the Legislative Representative Districts of the State to the scientific or classical departments of the college, and containing suitable dining-room, kitchen, matron's and servants' rooms. The natural conformation of the ground, and an abundant supply of water from the Maxwell Spring, render the construction of an artificial lake, with boating course a quarter of a mile in length, comparatively easy, thus providing for a beautiful sheet of water to add to the attractions of the landscape.

For the accommodation of students sent by the Board of Examiners appointed by the Court of Claims, as beneficiaries of the Legislative Representative Districts of the State, rooms for ninety students are provided in the dormitory. To these good, substantial board is furnished at $2.25 per week, payable in advance. Students lodging in the dormitory furnish their own rooms. Good boarding, with fuel, lights and furnished room can be obtained in private families, at rates varying from $3.50 to $5.00 per week. In all cases where students can at all afford it, boarding and lodging in private families are recommended.

AGRICULTURAL AND MECHANICAL COLLEGE OF KENTUCKY.—LEXINGTON

The necessary expenses of a student while at college need not exceed the following estimates. As a rule, the less pocket-money allowed by parents or guardians the better it is for the pupil. When supplies are kept short, the opportunity for contracting vicious habits is correspondingly diminished. Students should be allowed by their parents to create no debts. The necessary expenses for the college year are $133.50. The course of study at the college is very much like that of other similar institutions, except that a great deal of attention is paid to the really practical branches, while the course in mechanics and agriculture is exceptionally thorough. Provision has been made to assist students who wish to "work their way along" by a system that in reality amounts to a limited number of free scholarships. This is a college which is thoroughly in accord with modern ideas and the genius of our American civilization; and on that account alone it is assured of an ever-expanding growth and increasing influence.

Of all well known private educational institutions in Louisville, the best and most noted is the Home School, at No. 727 Third Street. Miss Belle S. Peers is the Principal, and the Board of Trustees is made up of the following gentlemen, whose names are all familiar: Messrs. W. Geo. Anderson, Joseph B. Kinkead, R. A. Robinson, Stephen E. Jones, John B. Temple, James W. Tate, J. M. Robinson and H. W. Gray. Miss Peers is a member of the Episcopalian Church, and the school is under the particular patronage of the Bishop of the Diocese; yet there is entire freedom as to the opinions and religious worship of the pupils. It may be well to observe that several different denominations are represented by the Trustees. Last year the Faculty consisted of fourteen teachers, and of the one hundred and twenty pupils sixteen were resident boarders. The chief charm of the school is the delightful air of home which pervades it, and the refining influences which permeate and radiate from it. All that is uplifting and

HOME SCHOOL FOR YOUNG LADIES.—LOUISVILLE, KY.

exalting is thrown about the young ladies; and the fact that the first people in Louisville send their daughters here to be educated speaks volumes for its high character. The class of pupils who attend here is of the very best, and the associations of the school are all that could be wished. There are a number of scholars who board in the institution, though the number is limited; and these find school life as delightful as the loving care and watchful attention of their teachers can make it. In regard to location, no adjectives are too superlative. Third Street is a magnificent thoroughfare, lined with noble residences and beautiful with spreading shade trees and spreading lawns. It is, in fact, an almost ideal city street; and the Home School is on just such a street as one would like to live, and in just such an attractive place that one would choose for a residence. All its surroundings are in keeping with its name, and it is in every way an excellent and thoroughly complete institution—such an institution as is fitted for the education of young ladies.

Cincinnati, Louisville and Memphis Line

The name of this line, to use a very slang phrase, "gives it away." It runs from Cincinnati to Memphis, via Louisville, and the distance between the two cities is four hundred and eighty-seven miles. The traveler on the Ellen N. has noticed, two hundred and twenty-eight miles south of Cincinnati, and one hundred and eighteen from Louisville, a small station with a number of side tracks. This is Memphis Junction, and here the Memphis road leaves the main line and runs toward the Mississippi in a southwestern direction. Much of the scenery on the route, especially in the vicinity of the Cumberland and Tennessee rivers, is extremely picturesque, while the country for the most part is rich and fertile. At South Union, eleven miles from the Junction, three hundred and twenty-nine from Cincinnati, is a strong "Shaker Settlement," with massive

BETHEL COLLEGE — RUSSELLVILLE, KY.

buildings, neat out-houses and extensive and well-planned grounds. The thrifty sect have a model farm and do a large business in canned and dried fruits. Of course, the place will well repay a visit. Nestled among spreading trees is Bethel College, at Russellville, Kentucky, while the beautifully-kept grounds around the buildings at once impress the visitor with the fact that the spirit of neatness and order rules in the institution. The location is excellent, and students throng here from all over Kentucky and Tennessee. For years the attendance has been steadily increasing, which in itself bears witness to the solid merits of Bethel College. One of its features is that ministers' sons and students for the ministry are given tuition free, while the latter receive forty dollars a year additional (if needed) from the Enlow Fund.

Russellville is a place of some pretensions; and its situation, in the heart of one of the best farming regions in Kentucky, is favorable to its growth and continued prosperity. It has a population of two thousand five hundred and is constantly growing. Bethel and Logan Colleges, and a theological school, are situated here, and it is a center of culture and refinement, as well as of trade.

⋆ Clarksville ⋆

On the East bank of the Cumberland, just above the mouth of Red River, Clarksville is reached. It was the judicious eye of John Montgomery that first discovered in the rugged hills that lie in the fork of these two streams a superior site for the location of a town. January, 1784, John Montgomery and Martin Armstrong entered the tract of land on which Clarksville is located. Armstrong laid off the plan of a town upon it. They named the town Clarksville, in honor of General George Rogers Clark, a distinguished soldier of that day, who was personally known to many of the early settlers of Tennessee and Kentucky. After the town had been laid off, the proprietors sold a considerable number of lots, and the purchasers being desirous that the town should be established by legislative authority, the General Assembly of North Carolina, in November, 1785, established it a town and a town common, agreeable to the plan, by the name of Clarksville. What became of the town common does not appear. It was the second town established in Middle Tennessee. The Commissioners appointed were John Montgomery, Anthony Crutcher, William Polk, Anthony Bledsoe and Gardner Clark. In 1788 a tobacco inspection was established at Clarksville. This was by an act of the General Assembly of North Carolina, and was the first tobacco inspection established in Tennessee. The fact is only remarkable as showing how early the cultivation of tobacco came to be an important industry around Clarksville, and as marking the inception of a tobacco market, which may still claim, with justice, to be the first in the State. In this year also the county of Tennessee—the original name for Montgomery county was established. There is nothing of the "mushroom" about her growth; and to-day Clarksville, as a collection of men, is one of the most solvent towns in the whole country. Situated in the center of a wide belt of the finest lands in the United States, on which is produced every variety of cereal, besides the great staple of this country, tobacco; with railroad and river connection with business points North, South, East and West; surrounded by an industrious, energetic and intelligent people, whose school-houses crown every hill and dot every valley—we say, with such a business constituency, Clarksville possesses advantages owned by but few towns; and her solid growth, from a trifling village into an important city, has not been accidental, but is the result of natural causes. The population of Clarksville is now about seven thousand, including the suburbs, which, from their contiguity, are naturally a part of the town. It may not be as large as Rome was in the palmy days of Augustus; but in the matter of hills it beats the famous "seven" all hollow. This is a thriving little city, and it is one of the great tobacco markets in the West. The river and the railroad have both combined to produce this favorable result. Then, of course, the adjacent country is celebrated as a tobacco-growing land. Clarksville is solidly built, and its business blocks and large warehouses speak very forcibly of its go-aheadness. The general trade of the city is ever increasing, and the commercial tourist finds it one of the most fruitful tarrying places in Eastern Tennessee.

⋆ Dunbar Cave ⋆

Chief among the attractions of Clarksville is Dunbar Cave, one of the largest blowing caves in the world. By that is meant that a steady stream of cool air pours out of it summer and winter its temperature is the same, and this mighty and never-failing draft is in itself wonderful and inexplicable. But the cave is of immeasured extent, and its possibilities as regards size are as great as Mammoth Cave. Each year new discoveries add to its extent, and it may be that the gigantic natural catacombs undermine the whole region. But be that as it may, the cavern is singularly beautiful and it has never-ceasing attractions for the tourist. Those who have traversed its echoing galleries, dimly lighted by the torches of the guide, have watched the play of the grotesque shadows flung on the walls by the moving lights, have listened to the resonant falling of the subterranean waters, and heard afar off the cry of some stranger broken into a thousand faint yet clear echoes, can never forget the impression made upon the inner senses.

But to return to the more practical affairs of life. The cave was discovered years ago, and held by its owner at such a fabulous price that none could afford to buy. At his death it fell into the hands of the present proprietors, who have built a hotel, improved the surroundings, and made the environments of the place all that could be wished. They have also taken some very commendable liberties with the entrance to the cave. Once on a time it was a mere hole in the ground; but, by removing the debris, which had been accumulating for ages, the entrance has been made grand and imposing. A magnificent arch of solid rock springs over it, while beneath is a splendid level floor on which hundreds can dance at a time; and they can dance there on the hottest day in summer, for the breeze from the dark depths of the mysterious cave forever keeps the temperature at 56 degrees. Invalids coming here find the air from the cave a great restorative, while Idaho Springs, but a short walk from the cave, are in themselves a cure for many of the ills of which flesh is heir to. There are five distinct springs of mineral waters—red sulphur, white sulphur, chalybeate, magnesia and alum—all of superior character, and possessed of many curative qualities.

DUNBAR CAVE.

The Cumberland is crossed on a splendid bridge, and then the road runs over the river "bottoms" for a long distance on a high trestle, which is far removed above "high water mark." The rains may descend and the floods may come but travel on the L. & N. will not be interrupted. There is a very pretty stretch of road along the river, which the iron track follows for nearly twenty miles, and then it runs through a broken country to the Tennessee river, three hundred and thirty miles, which is spanned by another magnificent bridge with an iron "draw" in the center. The view at this point is grand, and the Tennessee is seen to the best advantage. The country beyond is well timbered.

As we go South there are evidences that we are in a land of cotton. Cotton fields lie on the track of the road. At Paris three hundred and fifty-six miles, there is a large cotton factory. The town has two thousand inhabitants, and the three staples—corn, cotton and tobacco—are the exports. McKenzie, eighteen miles beyond Paris, rejoices in a population of one thousand, and has two colleges—one a Methodist and the other a Cumberland Presbyterian, a sect which is very strong in this locality and in many other parts of the South, notably Texas and Arkansas. This is the crossing-place of the Nashville & St. Louis road.

At Milan, three hundred and ninety-four miles, the Chicago, St. Louis & New Orleans road crosses. The town is rapidly growing and is building up finely.

⊷ Humbolt ⊶

Humbolt, four hundred and five miles, is slightly larger than Milan; and, like it, another railroad, the Mobile & Ohio, crosses the L. & N. within its limits. The town covers a great deal of space; but it is very pretty and attractive. Large quantities of fruit are raised in this neighborhood; and at Gadsden, five miles beyond, this is an all-important enterprise. Strawberries, raspberries, pears, peaches, plums, in fact, all kinds of fruit grow as perhaps they grew in the Garden of Eden. They attain a delicious perfection, and year by year more and more fruit is being shipped to the North. An estimate was made some years ago, and it would be much larger now, that in one year the people around Gadsden cleared sixty thousand dollars from their fruit-crop. Frost never injures the fruit, the climate develops it; and, what is just as important, the L. & N. furnishes the best of facilities for carrying it to the North and East. It has been found that farms which have been overworked and run out in the cultivation of cotton and tobacco, raise most excellent fruit, while this rotation of crops gives the land the needed opportunity for recuperation.

⊷ Brownsville ⊶

Brownsville, four hundred and thirty miles, is a large and handsome town, which is considerably elevated above the surrounding country. Its trade in cotton and other agricultural staples is large and growing, while its manufacturing interests are fast increasing. Brownsville Female College and the Wesleyan Female Institute are both situated here, and are schools with far more than a local reputation.

Just beyond the town of Big Hatchie the railroad crosses the river of that name. It is a tributary of the Mississippi and is navigable for a number of miles. And now the road runs through a level strip of country, past a number of small stations.

Bartlett, four hundred and seventy-six miles, is reached. It is more in the nature of a suburb than aught else. Then the track runs in sight of the National Cemetery, and its high flag-staff lifts the stars and stripes above thousands of soldiers who fell fighting beneath them. This great burial-place, with its massive gateways and splendidly-kept grounds, is at all times interesting.

⊷ Memphis ⊶

But a few miles further, and Memphis, four hundred and eighty-seven miles, is reached—the depot being almost upon the banks of the mighty father of waters. Memphis is a city which speaks for itself. In spite of two visitations from that dread scourge, yellow fever, it has continued to prosper. That which was imperfect in its sanitary arrangements has been corrected, and the unhealthy places have been made healthy. The stranger walking along its bustling streets, sees no evidence that the city has ever suffered in any unusual way. Everything speaks of activity and enterprise which has had the encouragement of success.

Cotton may almost be said to be king in Memphis, and cotton seed, oil cake and meal products reach an amazing amount. Then there is a large trade in grain and farm staples, while it has the wholesale trade that naturally comes to a great city. In a word, Memphis has risen superior to disaster, and is thriving and growing rich.

One of the signs of the times is the recent erection of the magnificent cotton exchange, which is one of the finest commercial buildings in the country. In this way the merchants of the city have organized methods of controlling trade and making it flow through their hands. They realize that the situation of Memphis makes an extensive territory of the most fertile lands in the world tributary to her; and that if they but make the effort the country will yield them its fruits and the men of Memphis are not the men to let an opportunity slip through their fingers. They are wide-awake, pushing and abreast of the times. Of late years the city has been almost entirely rebuilt, and it is altogether modern in appearance.

Its trade, both by river and rail, has steadily grown, and a wider field of enterprise has now been opened, since Memphis has taken to manufacturing its raw products, instead of sending them away to be manufactured elsewhere. Some years ago it was the general impression that the city was unhealthy, and, indeed, there were good grounds for this impression; but a thorough system of sewers and surface drainage has removed this objection. The death-rate and municipal tables of mortality show that Memphis is now as healthy as the great majority of cities.

EVERGREEN LODGE is situated on a northern suburb of the city of Clarksville, and is about to minutes' walk from the corner of Second and Wanklin Sts. The "Lodge" is the property of Capt. J. J. Crusman, on which is his residence—a fit abode for a millionaire—nestling, as it does among many fine specimens of evergreens, from which it derives its euphonious appellation. The fitness of the location for a nursery and flower-garden may be seen at a glance, from the fact that the magnolias of Florida and spruces of Norway flourish side by side, being in that happy medium of latitude where the rich and varied floral treasures of the South meet in gorgeous array their more sturdy sisterhood of the North. The flower-garden and nursery comprises about fifteen acres in cultivation. More than half is devoted to flowers. Carnations, roses, chrysanthemums, tube roses and dahlias are grown by the thousands; palms and ferns are also a specialty; geraniums in endless variety, and as good a general assortment of rare plants as is to be catalogued by any of the more extensive florists of the North. Large importations of bulbs are received each fall from Holland. Strawberries, grape vines, evergreens, flowering shrubs and fruit trees are all grown for sale and shipped at proper seasons to their numerous patrons in all the Southern and Western States. Five large green-houses, and a large area of glass in pits and frames is constantly in use in raising and propagating young plants for their respective seasons of shipment. Their catalogues are replete with information as to the treatment of flowers, and will be mailed free to all applicants. What the Champs Elyses is to Paris, Central Park to New York, and Fairmount to Philadelphia, Evergreen Lodge is to Clarksville.

The Tobacco Exchange building at Clarksville, Tennessee, was erected by the Tobacco Board of Trade, and is perhaps the handsomest building of its class in the State. It was built, in the best possible manner, of brick with stone facings and trimmings, and roofed with slate and iron. The building contains a large salesroom, lighted from the roof, as well as by windows; a handsome hall for general purposes, and eighteen rooms for general offices. It was erected at a cost of some twenty-five to thirty thousand dollars furnished by the volunteer contributions of the sellers and buyers of the market. Tobacco sales range from two millions to two and a half millions of dollars. There are nine stemmeries and prizing houses, who handle from three to six million pounds, according to the crop and prices. The tobacco of this section is composed mainly of those grades and types most popular in foreign countries, and but little is manufactured for American use. Under the progressive spirit of the age, which leads demands to seek the fountain-head as closely as possible, the representatives of nearly every country in Europe are to be found at this Board during the season, seeking to secure their supplies; and orders are being filled at the same time for Great Britain, Italy, France, Germany, Austria, Spain, Switzerland, Belgium, Holland, and frequently orders from Australia, Africa, the West Indies and Mexico are filled here, besides a fair amount taken for different parts of the United States and Canada.

And, speaking of tobacco, it is interesting to note the fact that its production is increasing year by year. Formerly it was thought that tobacco grown out of Virginia and North Carolina must of necessity be an inferior article; but this idea is now relegated back to the dusty recesses of once popular fallacies, and the fact is everywhere acknowledged

CLARKSVILLE TOBACCO EXCHANGE.—CLARKSVILLE, TENN.

that tobacco grown in the West is excellent, possessing distinctive and fine qualities of its own. Kentucky now stands at the head of tobacco-producing States, while Tennessee ranks fourth, with good prospects of doing better in the near future. In fact the great crop of Kentucky is tobacco, and its yearly value is $11,089,782, or just about one-thirtieth of the entire property in the State returned for taxation. According to the latest and most trustworthy statistics, there were in Kentucky 226,130 acres of land planted with tobacco last year, producing a total of 171,120,784 pounds. Think of it! Enough to keep an army smoking for a campaign of a hundred years! In Tennessee the average was 41,522, and the number of pounds produced was 29,365,052, the value being $1,538,757.

These few facts and figures show something of the importance of the crop, and the amount of capital invested in its culture; and, looking at it from a national stand-point, in 1882 the internal revenue receipts from tobacco were $47,391,989—enough to pay the salary of the President of the United States 947 times and still have something to spare. Not only was this amount collected, but 472,661,159 pounds of leaf tobacco were exported, which enormous quantity was valued at $36,624,357. These latter figures are taken from the census of 1880; and, as the trade has been growing, it is fair to presume that over $45,000,000 of "the weed" is now annually sent abroad.

The kinds of tobacco grown in different localities vary greatly. For instance, in Pennsylvania the great thing is "Havana seed tobacco," which, in other words, means tobacco grown from seed brought from Cuba. Most smokers are ignorant of this fact, and imagine that Havana seed tobacco means that the seed is in some way mingled with the natural leaf. In Tennessee the trade caters to the foreign market and the great bulk of the tobacco grown is exported, while the reverse holds true in Kentucky. And the most promising thing about this great industry is that the land suitable for tobacco-growing is not yet half utilized. There is still an abundance for the new-comer. And not only that, but the demand is ever greater and greater; for men will smoke, just as they will fall in love, and just as they eat their meals three times a day—and they won't stop until the crack of doom.

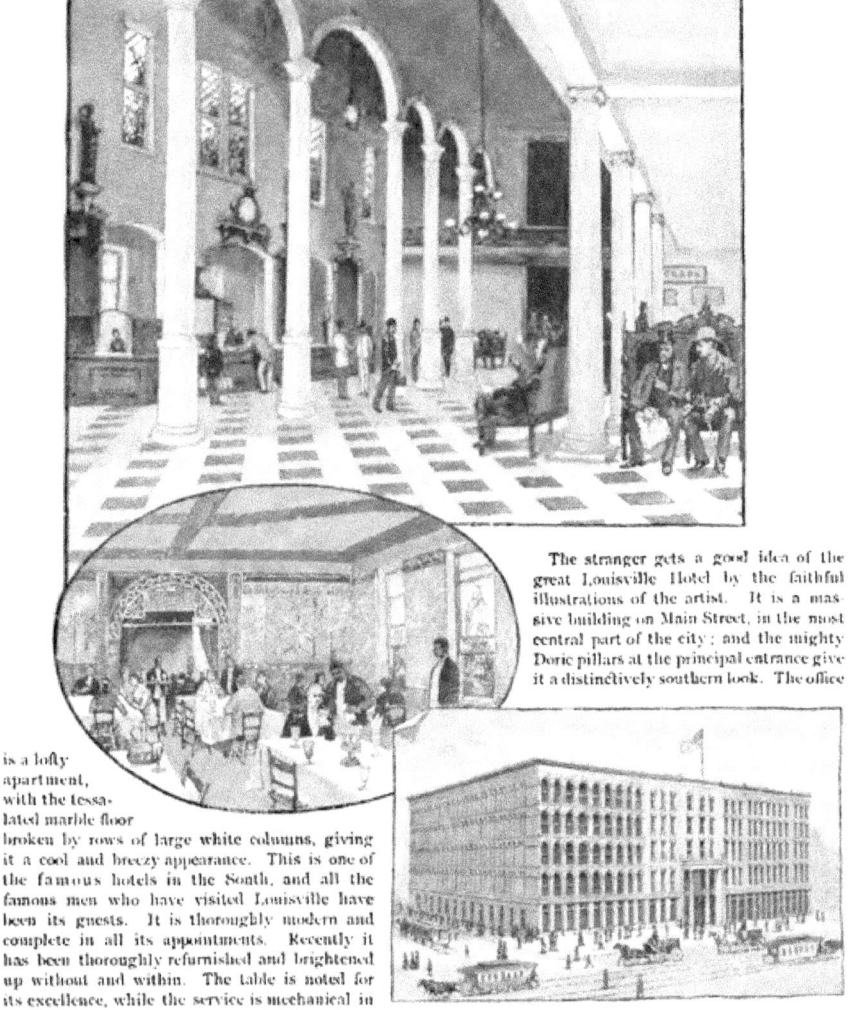

LOUISVILLE HOTEL.—LOUISVILLE, KY.

The stranger gets a good idea of the great Louisville Hotel by the faithful illustrations of the artist. It is a massive building on Main Street, in the most central part of the city; and the mighty Doric pillars at the principal entrance give it a distinctively southern look. The office is a lofty apartment, with the tessalated marble floor broken by rows of large white columns, giving it a cool and breezy appearance. This is one of the famous hotels in the South, and all the famous men who have visited Louisville have been its guests. It is thoroughly modern and complete in all its appointments. Recently it has been thoroughly refurnished and brightened up without and within. The table is noted for its excellence, while the service is mechanical in its perfection. Travelers say that half the charm of a place is in the hotel at which you stop, and this explains why the stranger at the Louisville Hotel finds the town the most delightful and enjoyable place in the world. During Conventions and Expositions the Louisville Hotel is the great headquarters for visitors. There it is that the political delegations get together and "fix" things; and the wire-pulling that has been done in the parlors of this hotelry is past all finding out. Many things have been done here which had made history for the State of Kentucky; and if these walls could speak the tales, they could tell of plot and counter-plot, and would be vastly interesting. During the war some of the most distinguished soldiers in our country stopped here, and at the broad halls and corridors wore quite a military air.

The Courier-Journal building in Louisville is not only the largest and most admirably equipped newspaper establishment in the South or West, but is also a grand and conspicuous public edifice, at once worthy of the city and fully adequate to the uses to which it is applied. The building is located on the south-east corner of Fourth Avenue and Green Street, in the very center of the business portion of the city. It occupies a frontage of one hundred and sixty-five feet on Fourth Avenue, and on Green Street a frontage of eighty-six feet six inches. The space covered by the building on the ground floor is fourteen thousand one hundred and seven feet, and the basement space measures twenty-one thousand feet. The building is five stories high, with a Mansard roof and corner pavillion, and measures seventy feet to the lower roof cornice, and to the apex of the Mansard roof eighty-nine feet four inches, and to the top of the pavillion one hundred feet four inches. The present Courier-Journal building was commenced July 14, 1874, and was completed and occupied on May 16, 1876. The cost of this magnificent structure, including the ground on which it is erected, was over one-half million dollars; and the pluck and nerve to put this large amount of money into a building devoted in the main to newspaper purposes is fairly indicative of the man who has made a prosperous and permanent success of the great newspaper of which he is the head. The fine business capacity, skillful management and untiring energy of Mr Walter N. Haldeman, President of the Courier-Journal Company, has made the Courier-Journal the leading newspaper of the South, and one of the representative journals of the United States; and also one of the best-paying newspaper properties in the land. Much of the prosperity and national repute of the Courier-Journal, however, is to be ascribed to the political acumen and brilliant writings of its editor, Mr. Henry Watterson, who is a leader among the journalists of America, and who has done much to place the paper he edits with such marked ability

COURIER-JOURNAL BUILDING.—LOUISVILLE, KY.

in the foremost rank of the great newspapers of the day. In the selection of a plan for the Courier-Journal building, Mr. Haldeman, who has always been a strong advocate and friend of every measure tending to advance the prosperity and interests of the city of Louisville, did not confine himself to what would simply supply the necessary space and qualifications for business incident to the publication of a first-class newspaper; but, with a generous foresight and deservedly successful issue, he has succeeded in furnishing the city of Louisville with a magnificent architectural structure, a monument alike to his good taste and far-seeing judgment. Such a building, which may have served the purposes of the Courier-Journal for years, could have been erected far below the actual cost of this building; but this alone was not sufficient to satisfy Mr. Haldeman as to what the future should be of the representative journal of the South and South-west, but with a liberality of means, as well as views, he erected a building upon a plan of unexcelled magnitude — a building unsurpassed for mechanical skill or artistic design.

Ah, what a city it is! A city beloved almost to the point of idolatry by its people, and which has a thousand attractions for the visiting stranger. Situated on the dividing line of the North and South, it is eminently Southern and yet distinctively Northern. Its citizens have the warm hearts and generous hospitality of the Southland, while it has the go-ahead-ness, push and energy that belongs to the North. "I think people," was Bea's sage observation, after we had been shown around the city, "who have friends to visit in Louisville ought

THE HOME OF "ELLEN N."

to be very happy. Why, here we have been visiting at the house of a friend and yet we have been treated like princes." But even the unknown stranger finds Louisville pleasant enough, for the hotels are excellent, and there is a warmth and hearty genuineness about the inhabitants that is reassuring. There was much in the city which we found entertaining. In the first place there was the town itself with its fine City Hall, Court House and other public buildings, while Fourth street has charms that are unfading. It is one of the finest residence streets in America. Not only that, but it has a character of its own and on that account can not be compared to Fifth Avenue, New York, or Commonwealth Avenue in Boston, or to the suburban drives of Clifton, adjoining my own Cincinnati. It is lined on either side by splendid residences, dwellings which for attractiveness and magnificence have hardly a parallel on this continent.

They are all detached and surrounding them are lawns as smooth as landscape gardening can make them, and in the summer time they are bright with flowers. A double row of trees shades this grand thoroughfare and adds materially to its beauty. At the end of Fourth street are the grounds of the Southern Exposition, which are well worth a visit. But Fourth street is not entirely given up to residences, as at its lower end it is a great place for business, and many of the stores are remarkable for their size and the completeness of their appointments. The Courier-Journal Office is on this broad avenue, and above its main entrance is a statue of Prentiss, the first great editor of the paper, whose mantle has fallen upon the shoulders of Henry Watterson. It is quite a work of art and it is probable that your Louisville friends will tell you long stories of Prentiss' wit and oddities. Certainly they told Bea and myself so many, that if I were to attempt to repeat them, this book would have to be enlarged to the size of Webster's Unabridged. Then of course before we left Louisville we saw the Falls of Ohio, which give the name of the Falls City, and the great canal which has been built around them. In high water steamboats go over the falls, but in low water this is altogether too dangerous a proceeding.

As to Louisville's enterprise and the extent of her manufacturing industries, I need say but little. Her thousands of factories, great warehouses and extensive freight depots speak for me. They tell of her material prosperity and wealth, of her commercial greatness and progress. And as a railroad center she has no equal. She lies midway between the Atlantic and the cities of the West, and is the geographical radiating point for the lines of the North and the South.

And now Bea and I, our visit at Louisville finished and my observations over, are en route again. This time for Nashville, Tenn., with a stop over at Mammoth Cave. As we slowly make our way out of the city, the train passes the immense workshops of the L. & N., where an army of workmen are employed, and then after passing factories, and rows and rows of houses, we make our first stop at South Louisville, where the through Pullmans from Cincinnati are taken on, and then we rapidly proceed on our way. It is a pleasant ride. At first the road leads through level farming lands, dotted with thrifty-looking houses in the midst of orchards and well kept fields. At Lebanon Junction, the Knoxville and Greensburg trains leave the main track. A few miles further and the country changes. We run through rocky cuts and around the crests of hills green with cedar. Now we are crossing a lofty trestle beneath which flows a clear stream, and as the train winds in and out we catch many a glimpse of bits of difficult and picturesque engineering. Meanwhile the porter passes through the car, and Bea exclaims:

"Look, brother mine, the porter is lighting the lamps in broad day light. What is it for?"

A moment after and we rumble through a tunnel and the mystery of lighting the lamps at noon-day is explained. Had it not been done we would have been left temporarily in total darkness.

◆ Elizabethtown ◆

One hundred and fifty-two miles from Cincinnati. This is the first important stop after Louisville. It is a thriving place with many industries, and is also a county seat.

Beyond Elizabethtown the country grows more and more broken. Wooded "knobs," or sharp pointed hills rise abruptly, serrating the horizon. The valleys make many turns and occasionally the land is flung aside by a bare crest of rock, whose jagged masses lie exposed upon the ground. It is a region in which Nature seems to have indulged her love for the unusual, and as Bea stands at the rear door of the car and looks out upon the landscape, she remarks that the only thing necessary to complete it is a cave. And the cave is there in Mammoth Cave, whose limitless caverns stretch away in unknown and undiscovered vastness, and whose thousand beauties and unprecedented extent make it one of the wonders of the world. It is reached from

◆ Cave City ◆

This is a little village eighty-five miles from Louisville and one hundred and ninety-five from Cincinnati. Eight miles to the west lies the cave which is reached by a stage ride, over a road which reminds one of the hymn the colored folks sang at camp meeting.

"Oh, de Jordan am a hard road to trabble."

It certainly is a rough road, but the tourist can pardon its discomforts, as the scenery is new and charming, and it gives him an appetite which is positively ravenous. But at the journey's end is an excellent hotel, a long, rambling, two-storied wooden structure, where the traveler is kindly cared for. A poet might rave over the untold loveliness and unspeakable mysteries of the cave, which is so rightly named Mammoth, but I am no poet. Let me say that the half was never told. No guide-book can do the great cavern justice, and no one can speak too highly of its wonders. I have never yet heard of a tourist who visited Mammoth Cave and was disappointed. No matter how great may be one's anticipations they fall far short of the glorious reality. You who visit the Cave can obtain volumes of information on the spot and your guide, for no one is allowed to venture in the cave without a guide, fairly overflows with narratives of the underground recesses in which the torch makes a "dim, religious light," and even the most inquisitive find in him all they can possibly wish to know. And you who do not visit the Cave can have no adequate idea of its marvels.

MAMMOTH CAVE.

As to the expense of a trip to the wonderful cavern it depends altogether upon what the tourist is pleased to make it. The L. & N. sells tickets to the Cave and return, so the traveler can at all times proceed upon a certainty. Not only this, but special rates can be made for parties and unusual inducements are offered in this direction. The rates at the hotel are exceedingly reasonable, not being based upon the fashionable "watering place" tariff, and the expense of a guide is trifling. Of course the larger the party the smaller the expense. Bea and I were with a party of six others, making eight in all, and one guide answered for all of us. We spent but a single day and a night at the Cave, and more time could have been spent profitably in exploring the mighty chambers which Nature has constructed with such massiveness in the very heart of the eternal hills.

"Well, Bea," I said as we regained the light of day after the everlasting darkness of the Cave, "what impressed you the most?"

Everything impressed me. Let me see, there was the Rotunda, the Tea Table, the Gothic Avenue, the Bottomless Pit, and that horribly dark and sullen river Styx, and then there was the Church with the Pulpit and Altar. I guess I was as much interested in the story the guide told about the Church as in anything else. It was about a beautiful young lady who promised her dying mother that she would never wed any man upon the face of the earth, and if she broke her promise all her fortune would go to another heir. And when she fell desperately in love, she came here with the man of her choice and was married with gorgeous pomp and ceremony in the Church. So she kept her word and her fortune, for she did not marry a man upon the face of the earth, but in its bosom. I guess that story impressed me about as much as anything."

As Bea is a romantic young woman she is to be forgiven. But everything in the Cave is so marvelous and utterly strange that it is impossible to tell what pleases one the most. As for myself there was nothing which did not charm me. Echo River is told by Emily Thornton Charles in charming verse:

ECHO RIVER—MAMMOTH CAVE.

Sunbeams never mystic river
Nor the moonbeams, o'er thee quiver;
Not the faintest starlight gleam
Shines above thee, sombre stream.
Night-enshrouded river Echo,
Mournful dirge so sadly low,
Loudly clear, or soft and low,
Singing as we gliding go
O'er thy waters silent flow
Comes the echo—" Lo!"
See the shimmering shadows playing,
Born of torchlight's fitful swaying,
Cast upon the cavern wall—
Cast o'er Echo River Hall,
Hear the echo call,
Answering echo—"All!"

And the boatman, standing grimly,
Throws a shadow weird, unseemly,
On the rocky space,
Strangely out of place,
As it were a network ghastly—" Lace!"
Bright-winged birds have never flown
O'er thy waters dim and lone;
Shores of earth with flowers o'ergrown—
Mossy banks, lo, thou hast none;
Only walls of solid stone
By the great Creator hewn—
By His powers alone,
Round thy waters—" Lone!"

Wavering shadows weirdly falling,
Seem as spirits beckoning, calling,
Calling through the echo voices,
Strangely awed, our soul rejoices,
As 'twere voice from heaven calls us;
Heavenly majesty enthralls us.

Now from dome and wall surrounding,
'Gainst the massive rock resounding,
Hear the echo
Come and go'
Long we gaze in silent wonder,
We of earth thou'rt gliding under
Through the rock reft wide asunder

O'er thy waters depth rock-girten
Plays the flickering light uncertain,
See o'er dome and caverned hall
Tracery of mystic scroll,
God's underwriting on the wall,
All His work, His—"All!"

Harken, now the voices singing,
All the echoes backward bringing,
As a grand triumphal ringing,
Every sense with rapture filling
Like a thousand harp-strings thrilling—
Every breath to silence stilling
Joy divine is o'er me stealing,
And a bliss profound
Echo tells me—" Found "
In the echo sound.

Long the sweet refrain will linger,
As the trace of fairy finger,
Rising now in fuller volume,
Answ'ring from each arch and column,
Joyous peals of music ringing,
As it were the angels singing,
Loud, resonant, rising higher—
Melody of heavenly choir—
Is it this I hear? Say, is heaven near?
This the spirit sphere? List the echo—"Fear!"

To my mind this truth is plain:
Know I now by this refrain
Words that die will live again.
And the grand resurgence rolling,
All my inner soul controlling,
Echoes ever o'er the river,
Stirs this thought within my brain
As long as a loudly-echoing strain:
Words may die yet live again.

Fairy river, gliding, going
Through the cavern, winding, flowing
To the wondrous realm beyond,
Here my thirsting soul hath found
Peace my longing soul had wanted
Quelled are doubts that ever once haunted.
Thou has taught me more than sages
By thy rocky cliffs of ages;
Taught me more than storied pages;
Led me to the opening portal;
Proved the soul to be immortal;
Brought of knowledge's mighty store
Hidden in mysterious lore!

Echoing thoughts my brain are storing,
E're unto my mind recurring,
Evermore this truth averring.
Thou hast taught by sure refrain,
Echoing dying words so plain,
I shall die yet live again,
Dying be my—" Gain."

MELLBROUGH'S HILL.

And now we again turn our faces southward toward Tennessee and the inviting country that lies beyond it. But the region through which we are passing is singularly picturesque, and the landscape is varied and ever changing. One of the most lovely spots in all Kentucky is Mellbrough Hill, which is circled by the L. & N., and of which a charming and truthful sketch appears above. The artist took his view of the hill from its base, where flows one of those clear, noisy, babbling streams so common in Kentucky. But in places the landscape is less bold and striking, and a softly undulating country is seen, which is dotted with white farm houses. Stone walls divide the fields, which look particularly neat after a dreary monotony of rough rail fences. The region looks peaceful enough now, but once it was marched over and over by the contending armies of the Blue and the Gray; and many were the fierce skirmishes in this immediate vicinity. And while on the topic of the "wah," as the colored people say, it might be remarked that this branch of the L. & N. played a great part in the campaigns around Nashville and Chattanooga. The road wasn't then what it is now, and the old iron rails and but indifferently-built road-bed were not at all conducive to fast time. It is said that supplies were over a week in going from Cincinnati to Nashville. In the first place they were taken by river to Louisville, then they were loaded on the cars and started for Nashville. What with bad rails, crowded tracks and few switches, and then the constant fear that bridges had been burned or track torn up, it was necessary for the trains to crawl. When it is remembered that at that time this was the only trunk line running North and South through Kentucky and Tennessee, it can be seen at a glance that its possession was of the utmost importance. Yet the traveler over the L. & N. to-day finds no reminiscence of that fierce and bloody time. There is not

OGDEN COLLEGE.—BOWLING GREEN, KY.

even the last lingering vestige of war. Were he to ask the train men of the battles along the route, and of the way the road was utilized to carry the ammunitions of war, it is probable that he would receive only the vaguest and most indefinite of answers. They may have heard of such things, but they are already ancient history; they are dead issues that are forever at rest.

The above institution reflects great credit upon Bowling Green, Ky. Ogden College was organized and established in 1877 A. D. by the liberal endowment of the founder, Robt. W. Ogden. The College is for boys and young men, and is fully equipped with an able faculty, and with all the usual means and apparatus of a first-class college, and confers full collegiate honors. By the wise and munificent endowment of the founder R. W. Ogden, and the bequest of John E. Robinson, education is offered free to any boy or young man from Kentucky, no charge of any kind being made, except a matriculation fee of five dollars per session; to students from any State other than Kentucky only a tuition fee of fifteen dollars per session.

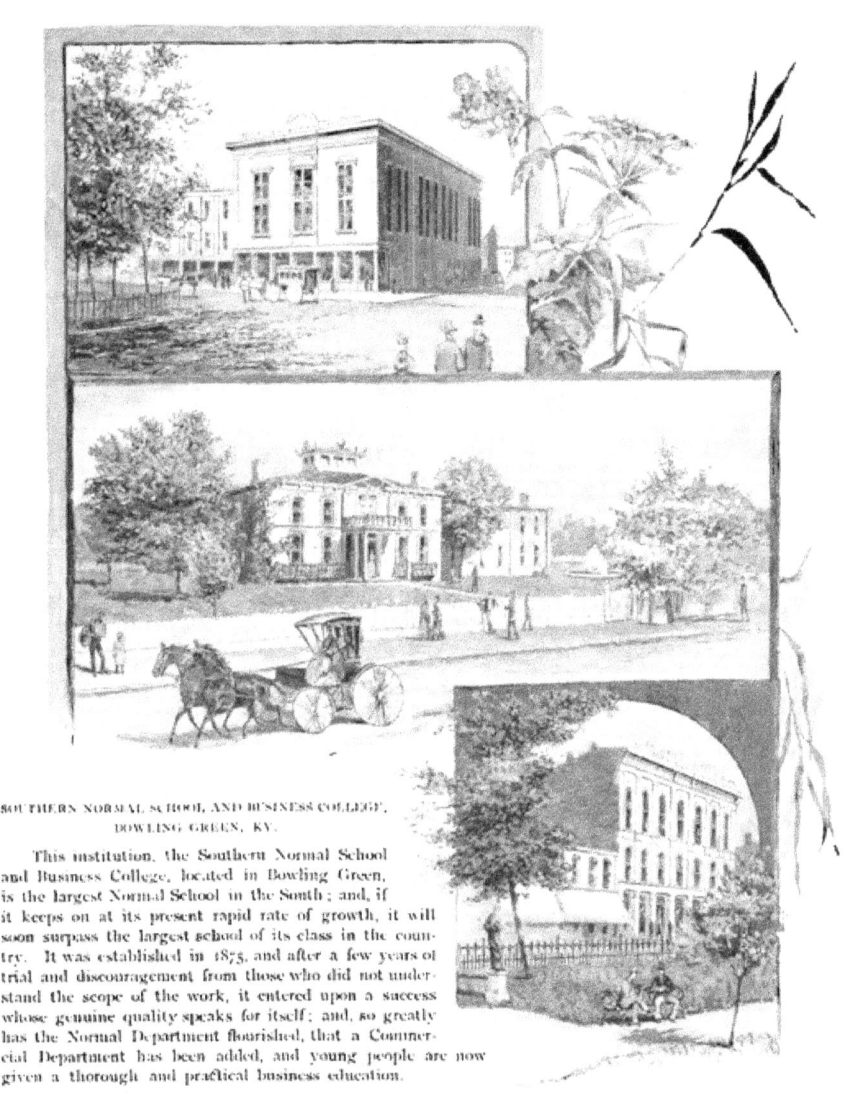

SOUTHERN NORMAL SCHOOL AND BUSINESS COLLEGE,
DOWLING GREEN, KY.

This institution, the Southern Normal School and Business College, located in Bowling Green, is the largest Normal School in the South; and, if it keeps on at its present rapid rate of growth, it will soon surpass the largest school of its class in the country. It was established in 1875, and after a few years of trial and discouragement from those who did not understand the scope of the work, it entered upon a success whose genuine quality speaks for itself; and, so greatly has the Normal Department flourished, that a Commercial Department has been added, and young people are now given a thorough and practical business education.

☞ Bowling Green ☜

A place dear to every Kentucky heart. And a charming little city it is. It is the home of many old families, and many of its citizens have risen to distinction and national reputation. It is a place cherishing genuine culture in its midst, and a home of education, as here is situated Ogden College and the Southern Normal School, two institutions with a widely extended name for thoroughness and general excellence. The little metropolis has a fine new Court House and a number of handsome churches. I say metropolis, and do so advisedly, for the thriving city has followed metropolitan ways and is supplied with all "modern improvements." Its Water Works are admirable, and the green mound of the reservoir, rising high above the city, is a striking and beautiful object. Bowling Green is also conspicuous for its enterprise, and it has a number of mills and manufactories. There is one handle factory alone, the handles being made of Southern hickory, renowned the world over for its exceeding toughness, which pays annually for stock and wages no less than $500,000. The river which winds around the city is the Big Barren, a poor name for a stream flowing through such a fertile land. And, speaking of the Big Barren, the question immediately comes to the mind of the stranger as to how it was named. The answer is simple. When the early settlers came to this part of the State they found it treeless. All the rest of Kentucky was covered with beautiful and thick growing forests; but here it was a vast and wide-extended prairie. It was covered with verdant grass, and great herds of buffalo roamed through it. But those old pioneers did not know that prairies were rich and fitted for agriculture; and, because there were no trees in the region they concluded that the soil was too poor and sterile for trees to flourish, and so they called the place the "Big Barrens." That they were very much mistaken in their ideas is shown by the fact that this part of Kentucky is as rich a section as is to be found in the State. Yet still the name of Big Barrens sticks, just as the name of the Battery sticks to what was once the Battery in New York, though for years it has been nothing more than a landing-place for immigrants. It has been pretty conclusively shown in recent years that the trees were burned off of this region by an immense forest fire, kindled, as has been suggested, by the Indians, who wished to turn it into a great meadow for the buffaloes.

Four miles south of Bowling Green is Memphis Junction, where the south-bound trains leave the main track for the great cotton and commercial market on the Mississippi; but more of this in another chapter.

◆ Franklin ◆

This is a flourishing town just twenty miles from Bowling Green, and its rival. The people of the two places are very jealous of each other, something after the manner of St. Paul and Minneapolis, but it is a good-natured, chivalric emulation. Franklin also has a good Court House, two excellent colleges and a number of thriving industries. When we left Franklin, Bea inquired of the Conductor when we would cross into Tennessee.

"The State line," answered the man in the blue coat and silver buttons, "is between Mitchellville and Richland. The first town is in Kentucky and the second is in Tennessee. No, there is no wall between the States and it is pretty hard to tell where one leaves off and the other begins."

And Bea was very much disappointed when she found out there was nothing to mark the boundary of the two great States. There was much more timber to be seen in Tennessee than in the State which we had just left, and when the pine woods of the North are exhausted, the lumber men will find a harvest awaiting them here. Already the lumber industry is very important, and it is increasing rapidly.

◆ Gallatin ◆

This was the first large town in Tennessee, and it is a thriving place, being an agricultural as well as a manufacturing center. A very imperfect idea of the place can be got from the station, as it lies back from the railway track, and trees and rising ground shut out the view.

And now it is but a few miles further and we near Edgefield Junction, the country becomes more thickly peopled, and at last Bea points out a grand building which lifts its lofty cupola from the summit of a distant hill.

"What is it?" she exclaims.

"That's the Capitol of the State of Tennessee, Mum," replies the porter.

And the great structure looms up more grandly as we approach it, while everywhere the factory chimneys and great business blocks are to be seen. Edgefield is just across the Cumberland River from Nashville, and while it is a busy, bustling place, it might be called an "overflow" town. The train only stops a minute, and then we are rolling across a splendid iron bridge, while the swift current of the Cumberland is far beneath us. It looks narrow when compared to the Ohio at Louisville, but it is no insignificant stream, and the steamboats which ply upon it add many thousands of dollars yearly to Nashville's wealth.

"But look," my sister cries and she is raptly gazing out of the window, "look at the long sweep of the River between its high, steep banks. They are almost precipitous, and see the great hills in the distance which shut in the horizon. Oh, it is lovely! Then just look at this Suspension Bridge in front of us which runs down hill. That's funny."

And it does run down hill, for one bank is higher than the other. But I hardly have time to smile before we are in the long depot at Nashville, and as we gather up our various belongings there is the metropolitan greeting, "Cab, sir, cab, sir'; this way to the bus! Express, sir, carry your baggage to any part of the city," and so on. Ad infinitum.

Nashville, Evansville and St. Louis Line

This line is three hundred and ten miles in length and passes through some of the finest land in all Kentucky and Illinois. There is a constant succession of thriving towns along the route. Leaving Nashville, the main line of the L. & N. is left at Edgefield Junction, and the road runs, as a sailor would say, directly Northwest by North. Springfield is passed and the Guthrie, where the Memphis road crosses the track. The line now goes through that portion of Kentucky known as the "Barrens." It is not called that because it is barren and sterile, but because of a queer mistake made by the early pioneers. The region was a vast prairie, and they ignorantly supposed that there were no trees, as the soil was too poor to bear them. Now, however, the country is well wooded, while the richness of the farms and self-evident prosperity of the region are sufficient evidences that it is not barren. Nortonville, ninety five miles from Nashville, where the Chesapeake & Ohio crosses the traveler sees marked evidences that he is in a coal region.

HENDERSON BRIDGE, HENDERSON, KY.

Long trains of "black diamonds" lie at the sidings, the coal shafts are to be seen, and as the train whizzes through the cuts, the black strata are visible, pressed between the gray shale and rock. Henderson is fifty miles further on. It is a large, well-built town and a center of trade for all the country round. Here the new bridge, spanning the Ohio river at Henderson, Ky., is one of the finest structures of the kind in the country. Its length proper is 3,686 feet; but the approaches, which are elevated on trestles to be above high water, will make its length in all four and one-sixth miles. The bridge proper is considerably shorter than the Louisville and Jeffersonville bridge, which is 5,220 feet long, but which is, with its graded approaches, only 7,750 feet in length. The Henderson bridge has the longest triangular truss

NASHVILLE

"SOME people," I observed to Bea after we had pretty thoroughly "done" Nashville, "find very little interesting in a modern, wide awake, live American town. I suppose they think they are too every-dayish, too new and all of a piece to have anything in them worth seeing. Now, what do you think?"

"I think Nashville is just too lovely. I don't know anything about the every-dayishness, as you call it, but I am sure we have found it very interesting."

"Just too lovely" is a woman's expressive way of saying that something is delightfully charming, and Bea hit the nail on the head exactly with regard to Nashville. I suppose most tourists, like ourselves, first visit the Capitol. As we walked up one of the hilly avenues leading to the building, we passed an old-fashioned Southern house, with a great veranda upheld by Corinthian pillars. There was nothing particularly remarkable in the house, unless it was its venerable aspect, but in the garden in front was a marble monument. There was a great stone platform in the center of which was a huge white block of marble, while four beautiful carved pillars supported a massive roof. We gazed at it from the street, then entered the gate, above whose iron posts is perched the American Eagle, and coming near the monument we read that "Beneath this stone rests the body of James Knox Polk, Tenth President of the U. S." This is engraved upon one side of the block in the middle of the platform, and upon the other side is an inscription briefly summarizing the life of the distinguished Tennessean. This modest house was his home, where his widow still dwells, and he went from here to the White House. Here he returned to end his days and here in the very shadow of his own home and the State Capitol where he first won distinction, he will sleep until the "heavens are rolled together as a scroll."

Then we passed on to the Capitol which crowns a high hill encircled by the city. It is a tremendously large stone edifice and every side is the front. That is, there is no distinction, as each of the faces of the buildings is complete, and all alike have a high, pillared portico, which is reached by massive steps. Immediately about the Capitol is a pretty park, with wide flagged walks and occasional fountains, while on one of the lower levels, for the park is arranged in a series of rising plateaus, is a statue of Tennessee's most distinguished son, also a President of the United States, Andrew Jackson. It is an equestrian statue of "Old Hickory," and it is identically like his statue on Pennsylvania Avenue, Washington, and the one in Cathedral Square, New Orleans. In fact, all three statues were cast in the same mold. It is fitting that the statues should be in Nashville, where he served his State in various capacities ; in New Orleans, which he so successfully defended in the war of 1812 ; and in Washington where he governed the nation and uttered the famous words which have since become historical : "The Union must and shall be preserved.'" This is the thrilling sentence engraved upon the pedestal above which the hero's steed is rearing in a very warrior-like style.

"Andrew looks very much as if he was going to slip over his horse's tail," said Bea, as she examined the statue. "Hush!" I exclaimed; "that is a work of art."

"Well, it looks that way, anyhow," she replied, with a woman's inborn persistence.

And while speaking of the most famous of Tennessee's sons, it is well to pause before his statue, in the shadow of the Capitol, and take a hurried glance at his career and the growth of Nashville in and since his lifetime. He came here in 1788, as public prosecutor of the Superior Court of the Western District of North Carolina (Tennessee then had no separate existence.) He was a young man, having just passed his twenty-first birthday, and Nashville was a wild frontier settlement, which was daily menaced by hostile Indians. It was in fact nothing but a collection of log cabins, with one larger and more commodious than the rest were. Court was held, and it took its name from one Nash, an early settler, whose dwelling stood on one of the high bluffs overlooking the town. As yet the territory was only a district of North Carolina, and there is a tradition that when the convention met at Knoxville in 1796, to frame a constitution for the State of Tennessee, Jackson proposed that the newly-made member of the Union should bear the name of the river flowing through it. Certain it is that before that time the territory was never called by that name, and Jackson may as well have the credit for its felicitous title as any one else. As public prosecutor Jackson was a success. And it required a man of nerve and vigor to bring criminals to justice. In the first place all the western counties of North Carolina were in a state of anarchy resulting from the ill-starred attempt to set up the independent State of Franklin; and then the constant warfare between the whites and Indians made men reckless of human life and regardless of the rights of others and the duties of civilization. But Jackson had been bred among frontiersmen; he was one of them and he knew how to manage them. He made a name for himself, and was sent as the first representative to Congress. In 1797 he was made a Senator to fill an unexpired term, and but a year later he resigned. Almost immediately he was made Judge of the Supreme Court of Tennessee (Jackson believed in holding offices, and plenty of them) and in 1801 he was elected Major-general of the State Militia. It was this last position which gave him the opportunity to make himself famous. When the second war with England broke out he offered his services; and in 1813 he set out for New Orleans at the head of two thousand five hundred enthusiastic frontier volunteers. He was ardent in the undertaking, and glowingly wrote to the Secretary of War that his men were not troubled with "constitutional scruples," but would, if directed, plant the American eagle on the walls of Mobile, Pensacola and St. Augustine, the main Spanish strongholds in this country. The first important action in which he was concerned was in the attack on the murderous Creek Indians at Hickory Ground, which is at the meeting of the Coosa and Tallapoosa Rivers. The red men were originally defeated, and afterward Fort Jackson was erected on Hickory Ground, which may perhaps account for the General's popular nickname. Shortly after this brilliant exploit Jackson was made a major-general in the regular army, and from this time his career may be said to have begun. The Government at Washington was badly demoralized, the capital itself had been captured by the British, and Jackson could neither get assistance nor orders. He marched to Mobile, defeated the English who fled to Pensacola. He followed them, stormed the town which the Spaniards surrendered after a weak resistance, and then he hurriedly marched to New Orleans. The story of the battle of New Orleans is known to every school-boy; and yet loyal Americans, who take delight in their country's glories, are never tired of hearing it again. The English blundered, and their two divisions fired into each other; then they attacked Jackson's hastily-built breast-works of sand and cotton bales, and found that their cannon balls were powerless to batter them down. The red coats advanced in long lines, and every shot the frontier soldiers fired brought its man; while the ammunition of the British was fired either into the air or the cotton bales. In brief, the magnitude of the victory is summed up in the statement that the British lost two thousand killed and wounded, while the Americans had six killed and seven wounded. Instantly Jackson was the popular hero—his praises were in the mouths of all. Well might he have said, after Byron's egotistical style, that he marched away from Nashville unknown, and marched back to find himself famous.

In a little more than ten years he was President of the United States. He was chosen as the champion of reform, though exactly what needed to be reformed is very hard to tell. But he set energetically about what in modern phrase would be "turning the rascals out;" and he made removals and appointed his political friends to place and power in a manner which caused the heads of the sober-minded, slow-going statesmen of the day to spin. "To the victors belong the spoils" was his maxim; and ever since his administration it has rung through American history with a continued protest from the party that is on the outside. This principle has been carried out by the Democrats and Republicans; and it is only in these later days that civil service laws and the plan of competitive examinations threatens to do away with the time-honored spoils system. During the first year of Jackson's term as President he removed four hundred and twenty-nine postmasters and two hundred and thirty-nine other officers, and, as the new appointees changed all their clerks, deputies and attaches, it is estimated that nearly three thousand office-holders lost their places. Up to that time the civil service had been looked upon as only moderately profitable, but a safe and permanent occupation. Washington, during his two terms as President, only removed nine persons from office; John Adams ten, and one of these was a defaulter; Jefferson, thirty-nine; Madison five, and three of these were short in their accounts; Monroe nine, and John Quincey Adams two, both for cause. Then came Jackson and his ideas about office-holding and office-holders, which were startling innovations. From 1787 to 1829 there were 74 removals from Federal office. "Old Hickory" beat this record in a month.

After his inauguration the capital saw what has since become a very familiar sight—an invasion of hungry office-seekers. They came in vast numbers, and their claims for place were based upon the fact that they had been "workers" in the cause and deserved all that party success could give them. This was the view that the President took of the matter, and his friends never had to complain that their services were not recognized and rewarded. Naturally, the administration strengthened itself wonderfully, and Jackson was never more popular—among his admirers—than when his first term came to an end. He was enthusiastically re-elected, and four years later was able to name his successor—Van Buren. In 1836 he returned to Nashville, after having been Chief Magistrate of the nation for eight years. He was received with all possible marks of attention and affection. His home was the "Hermitage," a country place about nine miles east of the city; and it became the Mecca for political pilgrims. Up to the day of his death, in 1845, he was bothered and pursued by office-seekers, who wished to obtain letters of recommendation from him. And his body still rests at the Hermitage. The tomb is of white marble, made after the style of the Roman Temple of Vesta, which stands immediately adjoining the old house. Bea and I made a pilgrimage

NASHVILLE BY MOONLIGHT.

to the spot and found that it was a vastly enjoyable visit. Everything about the place is as Jackson left it; some of the old servants are still there, while the relics are innumerable, and all of them are interesting.

"This is really as good as going to school and learning American history," said Bea, after I had told her this long story about Andrew Jackson.

In fact the man who goes over the L. & N. with his eyes open finds that he runs across a good deal of the most interesting American history. And speaking of history, Nashville saw some very exciting scenes during the late war. It was in 1862, and General Albert Sidney Johnston occupied the city with his army. Young, brave and chivalric, he was immensely popular, and the personal magnetism of the man drew many to his side of the struggle. All was going well, and the soldiers were reveling in the delights of city life. Suddenly came the news that Fort Donelson had fallen, and Grant, with his overwhelming army, was on the march to Nashville. Instantly Johnston withdrew, adjourning the Legislature to meet in Memphis. The day was Sunday, yet the churches were empty, while the streets were filled with excited crowds. The property of those preparing to flee was piled on the sidewalks, and by and by the throng degenerated into a plundering mob. It was a terrible time, and law gave place to anarchy. Then Grant came, martial law was temporarily declared, and Andrew Johnson was made Military Governor of the State. The City Council refused to take the oath of allegiance to the United States, and the Governor, enraged, at once removed them from office. The mayor was also obstinate, and he was summarily arrested. But what need to enter into details? That is all over, thank heaven!

Let us return to the live, energetic city of to-day—a city filled with fresh, live blood, and teeming with enterprise and which is in every way representative of what writers call the "New South." Like all other visitors, we greatly admired the splendid proportions of the Capitol.

As I said before, it is a noble stone structure and its corridors and halls are all of stone. The Supreme Court happened to be in session when we made our visit, and we entered the Court room and saw the venerable judges sitting in a row while lawyers and litigants were ranged around. But the most interesting place in the Capitol is the Library where is stored the collection of curios of the Tennessee Historical Society, and here the visitor can spend hours profitably and pleasurably. There are all kinds of interesting things to be seen from Daniel Boone's rifle, to the rough hickory chairs with which Andrew Johnson began housekeeping. Then there are battle flags, tattered and torn with many a long campaign, and every one of them has a history.

"I think these old silk dresses of the pioneer mothers of the State are more interesting than the flags," observed Bea, with a shocking lack of patriotism for which I sternly reproved her.

But the flags tell a story of their own and beneath their folds are ranged the portraits of many of the famous men of Tennessee. One of the pictures which catches the visitor's eye is that of Parson Brownlow, who during the war and immediately after it was as much hated as he was loved. He was a Knoxville, Tenn., editor at the outbreaking of the war, and was a great Unionist and fiery Abolitionist. He made his paper a compound of lightning and brimstone, and very naturally he was praised on the one hand and unstintedly abused on the other. After the war he was made Governor of Tennessee, and it was while at the head of the State Government that his picture was painted and hung in the Library. There are always a number of men, usually lawyers, here consulting books, and there is a hushed air about the place as in a church and the visitor goes about with muffled steps. When at last we had exhausted the curiosities of the Library we climbed up the lofty stone staircase leading to the Cupola. I say climbed, for it is a veritable climb.

"It reminds me of going up Bunker Hill Monument," I said as we toiled round and round mounting the top.

"Oh, dear," sighed Bea, "why don't they have an elevator?"

But the climb is well repaid by the glorious view that breaks upon the eye of the visitor from the top. Nashville lies at his feet, even the church spires being far beneath him; in the distance the tawny stream of the Cumberland divides the landscape, while all around the horizon is closed by the jagged hills.

"On nearly all of these hills," said one of the officers of the building who had accompanied us, "are the remains of earth-works and fortifications. During the war Nashville was fairly circled with rifle pits, batteries and forts. And part of the time there were gun boats on the river. The fighting hereabouts was desperate and determined."

"Many of the old soldiers are still living here?" I asked.

"Oh, yes, the town is full of old soldiers, Union and Confederate, living next door to each other like brothers. People up North have to come South to realize how thoroughly the war is over and its savage memories forgotten. The country all around Nashville during the war was made desolate, but now you would never know that battle and fire had ever done their work."

To the South we could see the red brick buildings and spacious grounds of Vanderbilt University, a wonderfully flourishing institution which was founded and endowed by the late Commodore Vanderbilt. And now let those who say that railroad kings and millionaire monopolists, as they call them, never use their money for the public good, be still. To the South-east is the University of Nashville, and to the West rise the stately buildings of Fisk University. This is for colored men.

"That's Jubilee Hall," said our escort, as he pointed to the larger of the buildings of Fisk University.

"Jubilee Hall!" exclaimed Bea, smilingly.

"That name strikes most visitors as mighty peculiar. You see part of the money to build it was raised by the Jubilee Singers, and that's how it got its name."

There can also be seen the Tennessee Penitentiary, which Bea and I afterward visited and enjoyed as much as a Penitentiary can be enjoyed, and the Custom House and Post Office, a splendid new structure.

"This is a grand view," was all Bea said after drinking in the beauty of the scene, and her words are as full of meaning as a chapter.

In going about the business portion of Nashville one realizes more than ever what a great city it is, and how varied are its industries. It is the distributing point for an immense territory and yearly it is extending its trade and increasing its manufactories. No one can ever accuse Nashville of being behind the times. The city is progressive, and is metropolitan in every thing.

It is a very closely-built town, and has more the air of the North than the South—that is, the buildings are not detached and have no suggestion of Grecian architecture about them. One of the finest structures is the new post office, which is as charming and beautiful as can be imagined. It stands "at the top of quite a ridgy hill, and its lofty situation adds materially to the architectural effect. Here it is, in the afternoons, that the Nashville young ladies come on a promenade; and one man who would dare to suggest that they are not altogether lovely has not yet been born." But, as a matter of fact, the new post office, which contains the other Federal offices, is exceedingly convenient and well arranged. Few Government buildings in the country make a better showing; and it was built within the amount appropriated by Congress.

But I must not forget to say that before Bea and I left Nashville we took a hurried trip to the Meade Farm and saw the blooded stock. There are some famous horses here, and elsewhere about the city are great stock farms. Buyers come from all over the country and the stockman can find what he wants, be he ever so particular.

VANDERBILT UNIVERSITY.

One of the most noticable things in connection with the L. & N. is the great number of colleges and seminaries along its line. Almost every town has a college and they are universally institutions of worth and standing. Of course the most noted among them is Vanderbilt University at Nashville, which is not only known throughout Tennessee and the South, but throughout the entire country. The site of the University is magnificent. It has seventy-five acres of land on gently rising ground to the west of Nashville, and the elevation is the same as that of Capitol Hill. By far the most striking feature of the landscape seen from the top of the Capitol, is the University and the park like campus which stretches around it, and while the view from this lofty "coign of vantage" is grand, it is not distance alone which lends enchantment to the view, for the nearer one approaches the more he realizes the extent and beauty of the University grounds, and the substantial excellence and architectural fitness of the buildings. Above them all is the main structure, or University Hall, with its grand entrance on either side of which rise two massive towers. Then there are Wesley Hall, a building of splendid proportions which is used for the Theological Department; Science Hall with its valued museums, drawing and lecturing rooms, while in the basement is the steam plant which heats all the buildings. The observatory is the best in the South and the apparatus is very fine. The meridian-circle room occupies one wing, with the usual roof and horizon shutters. The equatorial pier, built on a solid rock foundation, extends to the floor of the dome, free from connection with the building where it receives the cast iron base of the equatorial mountings. The dome is hemispherical, and revolves on a curved track, the motion being easily imparted by a traveling hand-gear. By means of a light windlass the shutter is opened by sliding it through the zenith. A tower in the north wing, with a revolving turret, is occupied by the geodetic altazimuth instrument. An electric clock in the tower, for use with this instrument, is connected by wire with the Dent sidereal clock in the meridian-circle room. A lower north window is provided with an exterior shutter-cage for the meteorological instruments, while the computing-rooms are on the first floor. The gymnasium has not yet been mentioned nor the nine Professors' houses, which are located about the grounds, to comply with the conditions of convenience and taste, and an equal number of dwellings for the Janitor, Superintendent of Grounds, and other employees of the University. Then the Medical and Dental Colleges are in Nashville, making altogether as complete and thorough an educational institution as can be found in America.

A word or two about the history of the college may not be out of place. It was founded in 1873, by the late Cornelius Vanderbilt, of New York, who on the 27th of March in that year, made it a gift of $500,000, which was soon afterward increased to $1,000,000. Seven years later Mr. William H. Vanderbilt made a special donation of $150,000, which was expended in building Wesley and Science Halls and the Gymnasium. But this is not Mr. W. H. Vanderbilt's only gift, as in July, 1883, he gave $300,000 which was to be added to the permanent endowment of the University. Thus, through the munificence of one family this splendid University has been firmly established and its future greatness has been put beyond the shadow of a doubt. It is growing and flourishing, and as an indication of its influence it may be stated that last year no less than 300 students were enrolled at the University, coming from twenty-five States of the Union and from Armenia, China, England, Germany and Scotland.

The great attention which is being paid to education is one of the features of "the New South." There was a time when the sons and daughters of Southern families were sent abroad to be educated, but now this is no longer the case. There are excellent colleges and schools at home, and the South is doing its own education.

We were not at all willing to leave Nashville when the time came for our departure, and as the train slowly steamed out of the city we kept our eyes fixed upon the lofty and beautiful Capitol, until a sudden bend and a high embankment hid it from our sight. Just beyond the city we crossed the tracks of the Nashville, Chattanooga and St. Louis R. R., and then we went on at the usual lightning express speed.

Twenty miles south of Nashville is the old and solid town of Franklin, in front of which runs the stream, Big Harpeth. The place has a substantial air of repose about it, and it is possessed of two colleges.

"There are cotton bales piled up at the depot," said a fellow traveler as he pointed to a great barricade of them, which were delivered here from the farms where the cotton grew.

In fact we had fairly entered the great "cotton belt," and as we proceeded South, cotton fields, a strange sight to Northern eyes, grew more and more frequent.

"Cotton is King," said Bea, as we whizzed by a cotton field much larger than usual.

"Yes," put in a fellow tourist, "but corn, wheat and tobacco, and in fact iron and coal are all members of the royal family, and each is striving for the supremacy."

"But cotton is King," persisted that obstinate sister of mine.

"Well, perhaps," said the other. "Certainly it is more king now when it is made into cloth and thread right here in the factories of Nashville, than when it had to be shipped across the ocean to make it useful."

Another twenty miles and the famous old town of Columbia is reached.

"Here it was," said I to Bea, "that President Polk began life. He started as a lawyer and his office was in a delapidated old log cabin, the picture of which is to be seen in the State Library of Nashville."

Columbia is a very old place and it has a reputation for business enterprise as well as for its educational advantages. The Athenæum and the Columbia Female Institute are both situated here, and if the tourist is as fortunate as Bea and myself were, he will see a crowd of red-cheeked laughing girls at the depot, awaiting the arrival of one of the companions. At this point the Nashville and Florence R. R. starts off for Mt. Pleasant and Sandy Hook, and over its rails is hauled the product from the iron furnaces of Lawrence and Wayne Counties. And now the road runs south through a magnificent country. The scenery a trifle monotonous, perhaps, but affording many glimpses of the life of the people who live away from the centers of civilization and events. There are log cabins by the track, and the women and children come crowding to the door as the train goes past. These are the "poor whites," not unknown to fame, and they are an interesting study. But the railroad helps them along and there is no excuse for remaining "poor" however much the accident of birth may affect them. Eighty miles from Nashville, or three hundred and seventy-five miles from Cincinnati is Pulaski, a wide-awake manufacturing town and the seat of Giles Male College.

Three miles beyond the little town of Prospect is the State line, which is only marked by a small station, at which our train did not stop, and so we dash into Alabama like a conquering army on a charge. Soon we pass Elkmont, where are situated the "Chalybeald Springs," whose waters are held in high repute for their medicinal virtues. It is a very picturesque locality and some day may develop as a watering place. As it is, it is much frequented. Then there is another stretch of "poor whites" who disappear as we approach Athens, a thriving town. Harris is simply the crossing of the Memphis and Charlestown Railroad. A mile or two beyond we crossed the Tennessee River, which is rolling on to Pittsburg Landing and past the memorable field of Shiloh. The bridge is a draw and is a noble structure. On the southern bank of the river is Decatur, a place whose situation will necessarily make it a commercial, and in all probability a manufacturing center. As soon as the Muscle Shoals are deepened, the carrying trade on the river, which is already large, will vastly increase. Decatur is fortunate in not only having the great trunk line of the L. & N. pass through it, but in also having the East Tennessee, Virginia and Georgia Railroad visit it. A few miles beyond Decatur and the country changes. It is very much broken, high cliffs and steep rocky gorges being the characteristics of the scenery. This is the beginning of the great iron and coal fields of Alabama, one of the richest mineral regions in the world. The possibilities of this country are as yet scarcely dreamed of, though year by year, capital and labor, animated by enterprise, are developing its resources. Just beyond "Sand Mountain," which is a marked locality in the industrial progress of Alabama, is

☞ Cullman's ☜

This is, or was originally, a German colony, and it is named for its founder. A few years ago and it was like much of the rest of the country adjacent, bare and unimproved, but now it has been made to blossom as the rose. In fact it is a pretentious little city with a Court House, churches, hotels, mills, factories of various kinds, a pottery, and even that invaluable adjunct of modern civilization — a brewery. Its houses are models of neatness and comfort, and almost invariably they are surrounded with beds of flowers. This is the place for the emigrant and the stranger to the iron and coal country to get his first impressions of the locality.

South of Cullman's the country is rough and wild, and the track goes through mountain gorges and pretty valleys. Then all at once, in the very midst of the mountainous uplands, we come to

Blount Springs,

which is four hundred and seventy miles from Cincinnati, and one hundred and seventy-five miles from Nashville. Here are the finest sulphur and mineral springs in America, invaluable in the cure of certain diseases. The air is a bracing tonic; and there are beautiful and romantic walks and drives without number, which invite to out-door exercise, and assist materially in the up-building of the physical man. The people of the Gulf Coast and of the South generally come here in numbers, and the number of the Northern visitors is steadily increasing. Hotel and cottage accommodations are all that the most fastidious could desire. It is no barren wilderness; but all that makes life pleasant

SAND MOUNTAIN.

abounds, and the society is always of the best. It is to be remembered that not the invalid alone comes to Blount Springs, but the mere pleasure seeker and inquisitive tourist as well. The springs bubble up from their eternal reservoirs in the hills, not far from the hotel, and their rocky basins are shaded by forest trees.

"These springs," remarked a healthy and robust-looking invalid to Bea, "are great institutions. I am the living embodiment of 'after taking;' but if you had seen me 'before taking,' you'd have thought I was the living skeleton escaped from some dime museum." "Not so bad as that." I put in.

"Well, not quite as bad, of course; but I was really nothing but skin and bone. The rest, the fare and the waters have built me up. I drink several gallons a day; in fact, I am a regular old toper, and take my drinks as regularly as I take my meals, and a deal oftener."

The waters are especially good in all troubles of the kidneys, bowels, liver, and the complications growing from them. They absolutely drive away a bad complexion and make rosy cheeks and velvet skin more permanent than all the "Lily White" and "Bloom of Youth" which ever was invented.

As I remarked previously, the surroundings of Blount Springs are beautiful. The scenery is charmingly varied, and among the attractions of the locality is even to be numbered a trout stream. Within a few miles are a number of extensive caves, rich with stalactites and ponderous stagtamites, and one of them has a mysterious underground stream flowing silently through its dark recesses. The "blowing spring," which is only a mile distant from the hotel, is always interesting.

South of Blount Springs the evidences that this is a great mining country increase. Coke ovens and smelting furnaces are frequent, while great piles of coal and reddish iron ore are at the railroad switches awaiting shipment. Even the soil is red with the superabundant iron; and when it rains the water rushing down the hillsides is almost vermillion. The evidences that the earth is being made to yield up its treasures increase, until at last we reach

⋘ Birmingham ⋙

the very center of the iron and coal interests of Alabama. "Why!" observed Bea, after we had had a good look at the "Magic City," as they call it; Birmingham looks more like an Ohio town than a Southern place."

And, in fact, Birmingham is not distinctively Southern in its architecture. It is almost entirely built of brick, many of the business blocks and residences being as fine as can be found anywhere; and there is an air of settled prosperity and push about the city that impresses the new-comer. Birmingham has not only a great present, but it is certain of a magnificent future. No wonder it is called the "Magic City." At the close of the war it hardly had an existence. Now it is a city, and its population and wealth is more than doubling every five years. All about it is an abundant supply of iron, coal and timber; and the iron and coal do not lie deep in the bowels of the earth, as is the case with the English mines, but it everywhere crops up above the surface. As one old miner said: "It is visible to the naked eye." The story that a man can take a pick, shovel and wheel-barrow, and go out in the backyard and dig out his supply of winter coal, is literally true. They tell a little incident here that is characteristic. An Eastern capitalist had purchased a large tract of land near Birmingham, and he came South to look at it.

"Why," he said to the seller, "I thought there was a mine upon it."

"Oh, that's all right," responded the other. "Here, John!" and he called his son: "go and discover three or four coal and iron mines for this gentleman."

This is not as big as it seems at first sight, for the hills which encircle the city are actually filled with iron and coal. The veins of coal in the neighborhood are from one to eight feet thick, and the quality of the article is unexcelled. Side by side with the iron and coal is found the purest and best limestone, while the hills above are clothed with the finest timber in the land. With such a wealth of resources, it is little wonder that Birmingham has so increased. On account of its great rolling mills, furnaces, foundries and machine-shops, it is sometimes called the Pittsburg of the South; and I think that its marvelous growth and enterprise demand that it also be called the Southern Chicago. A branch railroad runs from the town to the famous Pratt mines, which turn out nearly two thousand tons of coal per day. The L. & N. has on this line of road a grant of 517,000 acres all of it splendid mining land scarcely a third of which has yet been touched. Those who know told me that land in Pennsylvania, which would cost hundreds of dollars per acre, can be purchased here for a mere song. The L. & N. holds its land for sale, and, as it wishes to attract capital to the spot, its demands are extremely modest.

It is here that the Northern visitor will, in all probability, first feel that he is in the genial South. When we left Cincinnati it was cold and everything was frozen hard, while here the air was balmy and spring-like. Bea was compelled to lay aside her jacket, and she even wished that her heavy winter gown could be changed for one of lawn.

Beyond Birmingham the road runs through a beautiful country. It is very much broken up, and there is much to see that is decidedly novel. The pine woods have a spicy fragrance about them, and the ground beneath is as smooth as velvet.

"I would give a great deal to take a stroll through the woods and walk on the pine needles," said Bea. But the train rushed on and she must be satisfied to use her eyes alone.

At Oxmoor, six miles beyond Birmingham, are two large iron furnaces, and in all of the places hereabouts are smoking furnaces and great saw mills, with their miniature mountains of sawdust and broken boards.

"I don't think anyone ever told me I had a great head for business," Bea observed as we passed an unusually huge saw mill with a tremendously high pile of broken boards; "but I do believe that there is enough lumber wasted down here to make my fortune, if I could sell it for kindling wood up North. If I ever have to earn my own living, I think I shall start a kindling wood agency and grow rich."

"Great head! great head!" I say, and Bea proceeds to dilate upon the feasibility of her scheme.

Brook's Gap lies beyond Oxmoor, and through it we enter the Great Cataba Iron Basin, a region of unlimited possibilities. Silimia is noted for the making of lime, and that accounts for its name. At

Calera, the next station, the L. & N. is crossed by the Selma, Rome and Dalton R. R. At Cooper's, sixty-two miles from Birmingham, gold has been found on the smoothly-flowing Coosa River; but the iron of the region is a great deal more sought after than the gold. But who can tell whether some day gold hunters may not flock here, hungry for wealth, by the thousands; and the quiet banks of the Coosa be whitened by the tents of the treasure seekers.

Among the finest buildings of the "Magic City" is that of the First National Bank—a handsome brick structure with stone facings. This is the pioneer bank of this locality; and its steady growth and permanent success are typical of the progress of the region. When the banking house was put up nearly fourteen years ago it stood in the middle of an old field—now it is surrounded by fine buildings, while at all times can be heard the busy hum of the great manufactories which are making Birmingham rich and famous. The institution was originally charted Nov. 27, 1872, as the National Bank of Birmingham, with a capital of only $50,000. Its business increased rapidly and the need of a larger capital was felt. This happy end was attained in 1884 by a consolidation with the City Bank, and the capital is now $250,000, a quarter of a million of dollars. The business of this institution extends into all the adjoining counties, and its facilities for making collections are unsurpassed.

It is also well acquainted with the commercial standing of all business houses and information of this kind is always at the

FIRST NAT'L BANK OF BIRMINGHAM.

service of its correspondents. The present officers of the Bank, and who have done so much to make it a success, are: W. A. Walker, Jr., Pres't; John C. Henley, V.-Pres't; W. J. Cameron, Cashier, and E. W. Linn, Assistant Cashier.

Southward, and still southward, the country grows more and more level, there being long stretches of pine wood, broken by thickets of cane and holly, cheerful with its green leaves and brilliant red berries. Occasionally we rush past a cotton or a corn field, and finally Montgomery is reached, the Capital building looming high above the houses in the distance. As the train rolls into the city we look down from the steep bluff upon which the track is built, to the waters of the Alabama River.

❈ Montgomery ❈

It makes no difference when the traveler may arrive in Montgomery, he is sure to be received by a score or more of ragged, tattered colored boys, offering fruit or cakes for sale. They are queer little fellows and though they do not boast a single article of superfluous clothing, yet the garment or two which they do possess seems on the point of melting into thin air or vanishing into nothingness.

"I do wish I could make one of those pinckaninnies stand still long enough to sketch him," sighed Bea. But she is only an indifferent amateur artist, and the boys are such living examples of perpetual motion, that an instantaneous photograph is the only thing which would do them justice.

Very naturally our attention was at first taken up with looking after our baggage and observing the noisy little darkies. But we did not fail to note the beauty of our surroundings. The track is fairly upon the edge of a high bluff, which rises from the calmly flowing waters of the Alabama, and the river makes a great bend, so that the eye has a magnificent sweep. Almost at our feet was the steamboat landing, for the Alabama is navigable as far as Montgomery at nearly all seasons of the year.

"If you notice these colored people," said a Southern gentleman whose acquaintance we had made upon the train, "you will see they are different from the colored folks you have up North. They are more tropical in their disposition and take life with more sunny ease and carelessness of the morrow, than their Northern brethren. In fact, you are fairly in what is called the "black belt," which stretches across Mississippi, Alabama and Georgia, and there are more colored people in it than in all the rest of the country put together. Sometimes we say down here that we have too many of them, but time will make all things straight."

"I suppose," Bea questionly asked, "that nearly all of the older colored people here were once slaves."

"Yes, nearly all of them. Here in Montgomery you can find some almost perfect specimens of the old family servant, loyal and true-hearted they were, knowing nothing more in life, and having no other aim but to faithfully serve their master and mistress. To many of them the Emancipation Proclamation had but very little meaning, and they have gone on serving in the family to which they belonged without a thought of change. But of course that is not the way with the younger generation."

And in addition to the multitudinous, and if the truth must be owned, generally lounging negroes, the observer can not fail to note that Montgomery is distinctively a Southern city. There is a gentle air of repose about its wide streets and shaded dwellings that is suggestive of long settled comfort and aristocratic breeding. The streets are magnificent in their width, while there are shade trees without number. In the business part of the city the stores and offices are like those in any other city, but the dwellings with their lofty pillared porticoes and large windows speak of the South. The visitor can take a carriage and be driven about Montgomery and its immediate vicinity and see much more in a short time than he possibly could hope to do on foot. That is what Bea and I done, and we were charmed especially when we found that our colored driver only wanted a fair return for the drive, and did not demand all we possessed in the world, as is the case with our hackmen in Cincinnati.

I was told that much of the water used in Montgomery was from artesian wells, and that they had been sunk there with extraordinary success. I do not know whether it is the water from the artesian wells or not, but certain it is that Montgomery is a remarkably healthy place. It is also beginning to be a manufacturing as well as a commercial center. With unexhaustable coal and iron fields to the north of it, lumber all about it, and great cotton regions reached by its railways and the river, Montgomery may aspire to anything. And its people already realize the importance of its situation and are establishing new enterprises and reaching out in new directions.

Our stay in Montgomery was necessarily brief only over trains—and once again we are speeding southward. Before we had gone many miles the decided change in the flora and fauna showed we were really in another latitude and another and warmer climate. Indeed that latter fact was very apparent. Spanish moss begins to hang in greenish-gray masses from the trees, looking strangelyfully soft and light as it swayed in the wind.

"This is the forest primeval," began a young lady in the seat back of us, and then she went on, "with its ancient pines and hemlocks, beared with moss."

"She is trying to quote Evangeline, and say something about 'beared with moss,'" whispered Bea.

"Yes," I replied, "they all do it. Down here every tourist regards it as a religious duty to say something about 'beared with moss, stand, indistinct in the twilight, like Druids of old, with voices sad and prophetic;' just as up in the Michigan woods, the summer visitors all say this is the forest primeval. They all think they have struck a bran new quotation."

"It is very amusing," said Bea, and then both of us kept still and looked out of the window, for the young lady suddenly relapsed into silence and we feared that she had overheard us.

But there was not only the Spanish moss to show that we were down South ; there were cane breaks in the hollows, tangles of holly and laurel, magnolias and palmettos, with occasional oaks and always pines. Indeed, very soon the pines seemed to have driven everything else out, and to have monopolized the land, for it becomes one vast pine forest.

Greenville, forty-four miles from Montgomery, is quite a place, and numbers among its other advantages, two female colleges.

The pine woods seem endless, and beneath the ground was soft and brown with the pine needles. Evergreen, which is eighty-one miles from Montgomery and six hundred and eighty-one from Cincinnati, seemed particularly well named. Ten miles further south is Castleberry, where are Panther and Murder Creeks, two streams of some pretentions, and down them are floated logs and lumber rafts to Pensacola. It was here that an old gentleman, a native of the region, came aboard the train and sat down opposite us. Bea was commenting on the unpleasant names of the two creeks.

"I don't see," she observed, "why they didn't find some prettier name than Murder Creek. It's awful, isn't it?" "Rather suggestive," I replied. "That is a heap more pretty names than Murder Creek," put in the venerable old man on the opposite seat, who immagined that my sister's remark was addressed to him, "but then this here crick is named for cause, for cause." "And what was the cause?" continued Bea, whose sense of propriety was evidently utterly absorbed by her curiosity.

"That crick, long 'fore I was a boy," said the ancient stranger, "used to be called Turpentine Crick; and thar' lived on it a squatter, who, 'long with his dogs and his cattle critters, had a darter. She was a mighty purty girl, I reckon; and nearly all the young fellars in this here section kinder thought she was the purtiest thing on earth. But she jist went on a-helping her man in the house—a log cabin I reckon it was—and milking and making herself ginerally useful; and she never let on that she knowed she was any way purty out of the gineral run, or that the young fellers was trying to shine up to her; and she never said nothing in the way of encouragement to none of them. And when they'd go to the old

THE SUNNY SOUTH.

man, and ask for her, he'd always say: 'All right!' Whichever on' you gets her, has her. Whichever on' you gets her, has her,' he'd say. Thar' was one likely young fellar in the neighborhood—his name was Ross, if I don't disremember—and he follered her round purty nigh on to all the time; but she jist treated him like all the rest, and all the old man would say to him was: 'Whichever on' you gets her, has her.' Well, things went on like this, as I've been telling you; and all the time the girl got purtier and purtier. But I didn't start in with no intention of talking until we get to Mobile, whar' I get off, and so I'll kind of hurry up. Well, bime by thar' came along a surveyin' chap—one of them fellers that blazes the trees and lays off the country into squares—and the girl fell dead in love with him. This young feller, Ross, told the surveyin' chap to pack up his things and git. But I reckon he didn't intend to be bossed, and so he stayed; and he made love to the girl, while the old man jist said: 'Whichever on' you gets her, has her.'" "And which got her?" said Bea, who, I suppose, was growing tired of his rambling tale.

"Neither on' 'em. One day the surveyin' chap was found dead in the crick, with nigh onto twenty buckshot in his breast. That's the cause of calling it Murder Crick."

"But whom did the girl marry?" "Well, the feller Ross was never heard of after that, and so she didn't marry him, and she couldn't anyway, because she was dead." "Dead!" echoed Bea, aghast at the tragic tale. "Yes'm, she went and drowned herself in the crick." Then Bea was silent, and the aged passenger from Castleberry looked mournful, as though the story had been too much for him; and finally he arose and went into the smoker, leaving us in blissful ignorance as to how Panther Creek come by its name.

⛤ Pensacola Junction ⛤

Seven hundred and nineteen miles from Cincinnati, and sixty-one miles from Mobile. Here it is that the road to Pensacola, Florida, leaves the main track, and the through cars for Florida are switched off. It is not much of a town; there being merely a depot, a hotel, a half dozen stores, several saw mills and a number of houses. The tourist sees more railroad tracks than anything else; and if he is not going to Florida—unfortunate man—he can console himself by the thought that the orange State lies but a few miles to the eastward.

⛤ Pensacola, Florida ⛤

It is a very short run on the Ellen N. from Pensacola Junction to Pensacola, and Bea and I had scarcely settled ourselves for the trip, and chatting the while about the Land of Flowers which we were entering, before we found ourselves at our journey's end. We had passed Bluff Springs, Molino, which is more or less inhabited by saw-mills. Quintette, Muscogee, Cantonement, Gonzales and Oakfield. All of these places are given up to the making of lumber, and the buzz of the whirling saws struck our ears as we halted at the stations. Not only this, but saw-mills are scattered all along the road and they tell in no uncertain way of the greatness of the timber interests.

"It really is a land of flowers," said Bea, as she pointed to the gaily decked trees by the side of the road and then to the blossoming plants beneath them.

But while we talked, the smell of the sea came to our nostrils and the train glided into Pensacola.

This is the gateway to Florida for the tourist; and its situation and splendid harbor, which has but few equals on the globe, has made it a great maritime port. And there could be no more fitting introduction to Florida than Pensacola.

"They say," I remarked after we had come to know the place, "that first impressions are always the best, and if that is the case then the half has never been told of Florida."

"No," put in Bea, "what we have heard has only suggested its beauty and loveliness. I would be happy if I could only send a little of this balmy, delicious air home to the shivering folks in the North. You remember in their last letter they said the snow was a foot deep, and here it is like a day in June." "Oh, what is so rare as a day in June?'" she quoted with a laugh.

We set the town down at once as not only delightful and beautiful, but as a contradictory kind of a place. The old and the new is queerly mixed together. Side by side are the old Spanish buildings, which speak of a former age and generation, and the modern structures of to-day. The dead past, with its memories and traditions is strangely brought in contact with the ever living, business-like present.

"I didn't know that Pensacola was so old," said Bea to me one evening when the history of the place had been discussed in the hotel parlor.

"It has been here ever since the creation," I observed, but she explained that she meant something entirely different.

Almost a century before the Pilgrims set foot upon Plymouth Rock, the adventurous Spanish Captain, Panfilo-de-Narvaez, started into Pensacola Bay, and upon European eyes first burst that harmoniously beautiful picture of earth and water, of wooded headlands and shining beach, which to-day delights the tourist. That was in 1528, hardly thirty years after Columbus made his first memorable voyage. He brought back to Spain a glowing account of this wonderful harbor, and Spanish mariners visited it from time to time. Some called it Port-de-Auclose; others St. Mary's Bay; and still others Pensacola Bay, from the tribe of Indians which dwelt upon its shores. This last name was retained. It was not until 1686 that a settlement was made and then a fort, piously called San Carlos, and a church was erected upon the site of Fort Barrancas. It was a war-like place, always garrisoned with Spanish regulars, and it was the scene of many a bloody fray. In 1719 the French captured it and then it was retaken and taken and fought over until 1722, when the flag of Spain was again run up over the fort, there to remain until 1763, when Pensacola was ceded to England. The English did not regard it as very valuable acquisition, but they did one good thing and that was to lay the town off in regular squares. After the Revolution the town again fell into the hands of Spain. In our second war with England it was also a place of some war-like notoriety. General Jackson swept into it with an American Army, although what right he had to invade Spanish territory has always been a grave historical question, and an English fleet in the Bay destroyed Forts San Carlos and Santa Rosa, and Santa Rosa Island. It was not until 1819 that the territory was ceded to the United States, and in 1845 the State of Florida was admitted into the Union.

"That is quite a chapter of history," said Bea, when I had finished my narrative.

And we found it hugely interesting to visit the old Spanish forts and fight the battles of two centuries over again.

Across Pensacola Bay, a distance of four miles, is Warrington, where the Navy Yard is situated. I had seen the similar establishments at Washington and Norfolk, and Bea was delighted to learn that neither of them is as interesting as is this, not to mention the beauty of the surroundings. A landsman can spend days at the Navy Yard and never tire, while it has unfailing charms for the man of the sea. Everything about the place from the well kept lawns, war-like with piles of cannon balls and a field piece or two, to the docks and great work shops, is as neat as a pin.

"It is all in ship-shape order, I suppose a sailor would observe," commented Bea.

After we had gone over the Navy Yard, we strolled over to Fort Barrancas, which is immediately to the westward. Further on is the Pensacola Lighthouse, which Bea insisted on sketching because it was so graceful and striking ; and further on are the ruins of Fort McRae. A historic old pile it is, with a wealth of memories clustering around its shattered walls. But those walls were not broken by man. They were built too strong for that. It was the work of the waters of the Gulf, which gradually sapped the foundations. The visitor can find a great variety of shells here.

One of the most delightful trips about Pensacola is to Santa Rosa Island. It is a long, narrow strip of sand which lies across the mouth of the Bay and shuts out the waring billows of the storm-beaten Gulf. The inhabitants call it a "sand-key." It has a magnificent beach, where the finest surf bathing in the world may be enjoyed. The waves come rolling up the long, smooth white incline a hundred feet or more.

This beach is the incubator of the great turtles of the Gulf. Its gradual incline, the easily excavated sand beyond, and the warm southern exposure, adapt it to their approach, the making of nests and hatching of their eggs. So they resort to it for this purpose, and in due time the young turtles are hatched, unless the eggs are captured by various creatures, biped and quadruped, who seek them in the season. From Pensacola over to the island is about seven miles, and as the land breeze of the night sets fair across the bay, it is a pleasant trip of moonlight nights to run over on a sail boat, land on the bay shore, walk across the island, which is not a third of a mile wide opposite the city, and seek for "turtle crawls" on the Gulf beach, or bathe luxuriously in the surf. The "crawl" shows on the sand where the under shell has been dragged along, and following this up to a point above the wash of the

PENSACOLA BAY.

highest waves, the nest is found, usually about two and a half feet below the surface. A single nest will contain from one hundred to three hundred eggs. At Sabine Pass, on Santa Rosa Island, alligators are found by the ten thousand, and are killed in large numbers by the hunters who frequent the place.

The fishing off the island is, as a veteran angler said, immense, and the Santa Rosa "red snapper banks" are known all over the South. I don't know whether it is pleasanter to catch red snapper or eat them, but certain it is that it is glorious, nerve-thrilling sport to haul in the great, rosy fish almost as fast as you can play your line. Then there is the gamely salt water trout and Spanish mackerel which afford excellent sport. Speaking of fishing I must not forget to say that fresh water fish abound in the net work of bayous, rivers and streamlets which surround Pensacola. There is as much genuine sport in catching them as in hooking fish in the waters of Northern Michigan, and you catch ten here to one there.

All around excursions invite the tourist. After Santa Rosa Island and a visit to Fort Pickens, comes a trip to Escambia Bay and the river of the same name. Then there is Pulido Bay which is only less lovely than Escambia Bay, though both are beautiful beyond description. A voyage up Escambia River which winds in and out with many a turn and convolution, is pleasurable. The little steamer in some places brushes through the foliage of the overhanging trees, and then again the shore is hugged so closely that it would be an easy matter to step from the deck of the moving boat to *terra firma*.

But this is only one of many enjoyable excursions. West Florida abounds with uniquely beautiful places and scenery which is unequaled. The tourist may come here with great expectations, but he will find them more than realized. And for a trip through Florida there could be no better base of operations than Pensacola. In other parts of this book can be found a list of the Florida steamboat lines and railways, and the traveler will have no difficulty in selecting his route. Twenty different routes are open to him, and wherever he goes he will find this land of flowers and tropical fruits, this land of balmy breezes and genial sunshine, this land of health and physical well-being, attractive and new. The Florida tourist is never disappointed. Thousands of people from the North have come here expecting to spend a week or two, and their stay has lengthened into months. The winter cottages in Pensacola, of many Northerners who spend half the year here, tell more forcibly than words of mine, the attractiveness of this favored region.

If the stranger wishes to follow in Bea's and my footsteps, he will take the Pensacola and Atlantic Railroad to Chatahoochee, (which is pronounced with three sneezes and a shiver) thence to Tallahassee, capitol of the State, then east to Jacksonville, and down the St. John's River to Polatka and St. Augustine. That is a delightful trip. It takes one through the great orange country, and past the most characteristic Florida scenery. Then we returned via Cedar Keys and across the Gulf to Pensacola. We might have gone south to Key West and on to Havana, Cuba, which latter port is only five hundred and ten miles from Pensacola.

Leaving Pensacola Junction the road runs through the same vast pine woods, and before long comes to Canoe. It is noted for its turpentine interests, and much capital and labor is employed in the manufacture of turpentine and rosin. Fortunes have been made in this business, and few Northerners have any idea as to its extent. An ordinary turpentine factory turns out between 5,000 and 10,000 barrels of rosin per year, and for each 5,000 barrels of rosin there are 800 barrels of turpentine. It must be remembered that a turpentine barrel is nearly twice as large as a rosin barrel.

And now we go through a country that is very strange to our eyes. There are long stretches of level, marshy land where the vegetation grows luxuriantly thick and wild; where pendant vines hang from tree to tree making tangled arcades; but which are never traversed by the feet of man. Then comes a bit of higher ground, and the next moment the train is rumbling over an arm of the Mobile Bay, or over a river whose calm and sluggish waters seem to be drowsy.

Tall rushes grow by their banks, unknown reeds lift themselves from the mud and the eminently tropical palmetto is everywhere. Gradually the country becomes a dead level, the smell of salt water comes to our nostrils and on and on until our train glides into Mobile.

The City of Live Oaks, and it is rightly named. As soon as one leaves the busy commercial center of the city, the streets widen into magnificent avenues, shaded by long rows of the ever verdant live oaks, and lined with great Southern houses, reveling in veranda on veranda, and pillared portico on pillared portico. And the windows are so breezily open and the doors of such a generous and hospitable width that one feels that this must be the land of sunshine and flowers. At least Bea and I were very positive about it. Here the grass was a glorious green, and magnolias, figs and orange trees, mulberries and the umbella china were rich in their never failing foliage. But a few short days before in Cincinnati everything was bleak and bare, and here seven hundred and eighty miles south, the winds bore with them the freshness of Spring, birds were singing and life seemed a delicious dream of light and warmth.

Every year Mobile is becoming better known to the tourist. Those who are fleeing from the blizzards which blow with such icy fierceness from the snowy winter wastes of Dakota, here find shelter, balminess and all the comforts of civilized and urban life. There is the splendid "shell" road for driving, the Bay for sailing, theaters for amusement, and churches without number. And the delights of living are enhanced by the oysters from the Bay, which experienced and professional epicures pronounce to be par excellence. Of course Bea and I tried them, not once but often, and as I write of those delicious bivalves which go slipping down one's throat as though they enjoyed being eaten, I think of the song

"Her sweet smile haunts me still."

Those oysters still make my mouth water.

Mobile is at the head of the Bay which bears its name, and here the Mobile River, a slow and sleepy stream, empties its waters. The Mobile River, by the way, is quite eccentric. It is formed by the junction of the Alabama and a river which bears the remarkable name of Tombigbee, and after flowing south a few miles it divides, the eastern branch being called the Tensas, but before long the divided river again unites. The Bay is indeed beautiful, and a sail over its waves is delightful. I had been reading up on Mobile, and as we glided over the waters in front of the city, I told Bea the story of Iberville and his brother Bierville.

"They were Canadians," I said, "and nearly two centuries ago they left Canada, or New France as it was then called, and sailed down the Atlantic Coast into the Gulf to form a settlement on the Mississippi. They crept along the coast until they came to Pensacola Harbor. There was a Spanish settlement here, and the Commander received them graciously enough but would not permit them to land, so they sailed on until they reached Mobile Bay. They first landed on a large island on which they found piles on piles of bleached human bones. So they called it Massacre Island, though now it is known as Dauphine Island."

"Were they white men's bones?" inquired Bea, interrupting my historical narrative.

"No, I guess they belonged to Indians who had gone to the Happy Hunting Grounds. The Mobile Indians dwelt here, and as they had the disagreeable habit of cooking and eating their captives, the bones may have signalized the cannibalistic rejoicings after some great victory. That was in 1702, and in the same year Bierville built a fort about twenty miles up the Mobile River on the west bank. The situation was out

A SOUTHERN HOME.

of the way however, and so he finally started the settlement which has grown into Mobile. They tell a very funny story about the "petticoat insurrection" which took place in 1706."

"Do you mean to say there was a rebellion among the women?" asked Bea, with a look of interest.

"That's just about it. You see the ladies of the Colony were very dainty and delicate, and they rebelled because they were obliged to eat Indian corn." "And how did it end?" said my sister.

"I believe the women were forced to yield; starved into it, perhaps. Or else they learned how to make corn bread and corn cakes; and so their sorrow was turned into rejoicing."

"Then it was in this Bay," I continued, "that Farragut won immortal fame. It was on the fifth day of August, 1864, that the Union fleet began the attack. At the entrance to the Bay the Confederates had Fort Morgan on one side and Fort Gaines on the other, while in the Bay beyond lay a number of small iron-clads, ready for action. The Union ships resolved to make a dash of it, and they steamed into the Bay under a terrible fire from the forts, which they returned with very little effect. Just as the Tecumseh, one of the largest of the vessels, came opposite Fort Morgan, it struck a torpedo and almost immediately sunk. Thereupon the Brooklyn, another large ship, began to back, and threw the rest of the fleet in confusion. Her commander evidently thought he was in a hot place, and that it was almost time to 'git.' He signalled to Farragut: 'We have just lost our best monitor. What shall I do?' Farragut, who was lashed in the rigging of his flag-ship, the Hartford, sent back the brief but unmistakable message, 'Go ahead!'" "And did they go ahead?"

"Yes; they passed the forts, captured the fleet in the Bay, and took Mobile."

We found a visit to the grass-grown fortifications filled with interest; but "grim-visaged war had smoothed his wrinkled front," and put on such a peaceful, happy smile that it was hard to realize that here blood had flowed like water, and deeds were wrought which will go ringing down the ages. Massacre

Island a second time deserved its name. But the past is past. Heaven be thanked! And as Bea and I sat near one of the old forts, and gazed out upon the ships in the roadstead, the war, with all its horrid tumult, seemed centuries distant.

The entrance to the Bay is about two and one-half miles in width, and it is completely land-locked. It is one of the magnificent harbors of the world. There is a distance of about twelve miles from the Gulf to Mobile and, as the Bay shallows toward the further end, the largest ships can not be loaded at the Mobile wharves. But the channel is being rapidly deepened, and this fault will speedily be remedied.

"The stretch of road between Mobile and New Orleans," remarked a socially inclined old gentleman to Bea, when we had taken the train to continue our journey, "is one of the most beautiful in all the country. You won't find any lofty mountains on it, any deeply cut canyons, or any Swiss valleys. This is not a region where Nature displays her wild and ruggedly massive strength. I won't call the scenery sublime, but it is beautiful and it is entirely new. Then the road itself is remarkable. In some places it is built across bottomless morasses and swamps where the land and water meet and fight for possession. It is really a wonderful triumph of engineering skill, and the men who built it deserve all credit."

This was what the old gentleman said and he fell far short of the truth. For one hundred and forty miles the road skirts the Gulf, sometimes running on the very beach, now crossing a bayou or cutting right across one of the numerous arms of the great inland sea, or again traversing an endless swamp whose green reeds stretch away on unbroken level like a limitless prairie. And nearly always the dancing waves of the "Mexique Gulf" are in sight. On a fair day when the heavens are blue and sun bright above, when the earth is divinely green and the waters are all aglow below, the ride is one of pure delight. And, tourist, let me warn you. If the day be dark and heavy clouds blacken the sky, while the Gulf is rough and troubled, you will not find the scenery attractive. The smooth road and splendid cars will make the ride pleasant of course, but that part of the entertainment which nature is expected to furnish will be woefully lacking.

Some parts of the region remind me of the observation made by a cynical cuss from Boston. He said: "This section was only half made up by the Lord, when man came along and claimed possession. Ever since then the Lord hasn't meddled and man has been left to get along as best as he can."

But that is a very absurd criticism. It is a fortunate thing that the Lord didn't make the world alike. And that part of Louisiana and Mississippi and the Gulf plays just as important a part in the economy of nature as New England itself. Still, to stop this philosophical discussion, Bea called my attention to the fact that the first station after Mobile was called Venetia.

"It is a very appropriate name," she said, "seeing that there is more water to be seen than land." And then she went on to remark that the station after that was called St. Elmo, and that she had read a charming novel of that name. I tried to tell her about the St. Elmo lights, and she proceeded at the same time to tell about the novel, until we suddenly realized how ridiculous it all was, and fell to gazing out of the car windows. For some miles the road runs by the shore of the Mobile Bay, and we caught glimpses of the shipping at the wharves, and of the vessels lying at anchor far out on the waters. There were a few fleecy clouds in the sky, and these cast their shadows upon the Bay. Now a ship would gleam in the sunlight, all her masts and yard glistening like polished gold; then the long shadow would drift down, and the ships would suddenly grow dark and lifeless, only to be again gloriously transformed.

"Ah!" half sighed Bea, "I wonder if Farragut noticed how beautiful it was when he sailed up the Bay."

"No, I don't think he did. If he thought of anything except the details of the battle, it was probably of the torpedoes, with which it was said the Bay was filled, and which at any time might blow his flag-ship and all her crew into kingdom come."

Grand Bay is a beautiful place, and the views around are magnificent. It is a great shipping point for telegraph poles and sticks suitable for "pile-driving." Great heaps of this timber are piled up everywhere, and the air smells fresh and resinous.

Fifteen miles beyond Grand Bay is Scranton, while immediately adjoining it is the town of East Pascagoula; and this is another great lumber point. The long bridge which the train crosses is over the Pascagoula River, and lumber is floated down the stream and its branches in almost unlimited quantities. There are great saw mills in sight, and mountains of sawdust tell a tale of industry that needs no complimentary adjectives.

As Bea and I looked out from the train, we could see far away ships upon the horizon, while off from the coast were two islands, Turtle and Horn. They looked dim and hazy, and an inexperienced landsman would hardly have known that they were islands, unless told.

"I would really like to know if this land has any value," observed Bea, when we were fairly out of Scranton, and were skimming across an apparently endless marsh, which is every now and then broken by the lazy waters of some bayou.

"You're a stranger here, Miss?" inquired a passenger across the aisle, and whose baggage proclaimed him a resident of New Orleans. "Yes," she replied. "From Cincinnati," I added.

"Well, I guess you don't have much of this kind of land up there. But you asked if it had any value. Of course it is not laid out in building lots, and I never heard of any crops being raised on it; but in summer it brings forth just about the biggest mosquitoes in the world. They used to say, when this road was building, they never could leave any of the rails or crowbars round loose, as the skeeters'd use them to pick their teeth. I guess that is a yarn, however. Still, they tell the story, and I give it for what it is worth." "Then a man might have a pretty large landed estate in this region and still not be very rich?" continued that inquisitive girl. "Yes, that is so. But there is one thing for which these swamps are celebrated, and that is the shooting upon them. In certain seasons of the year they are fairly alive with wild ducks and water fowl of various varieties. Sportsmen come from all over the country, and if a man doesn't bag all the game he can carry away in a baggage car, it is because he has never learned how to pull the trigger."

Then we arrived at West Pascagoula, which is four miles from Scranton, or eight hundred and twenty-four from Cincinnati, and the gentleman from New Orleans began to tell us of the "Creosoting" works which are

THE HOME OF JEFFERSON DAVIS.

situated here. Creosoting is a process by which timbers that are to be driven into water infested with boring, gnawing sea worms, are rendered absolutely safe from their insidious attacks. In brief, the sticks of timber to be treated are placed in a large iron cylinder which is then closed, and by an ingenious plan they are thoroughly saturated with creosote. The works "smell to heaven," for creosote is anything but savory. But West Pascagoula is quite a winter resort, and the beach is lined with bath houses, while pretty pleasure yachts mingle with the oyster boats and still less aristocratic crafts which are to be seen upon the Gulf. And now we come to Ocean Springs, on the east side of the Bay of Biloxi, while on the further side lies the famous old town of

◄ Biloxi ►

once the capitol of the golden province of "La Louisane," when "La Belle France" was just beginning to establish her empire in the New World. Here it was that Iberville, in 1699, anchored his ships and tried in vain to patch up an alliance, offensive and defensive, with the timid Biloxi Indians. His brother Bierville, of whom I have already spoken, founded the town. When the great Mississippi Co. was chartered in France in 1712, the most extravagant expectations were held in regard to Biloxi, and it was hoped that great stores of gold and pearls' could be obtained from the favored locality. The prospectors, as they would be called at the present time out west, wrote back that there was neither gold nor pearls, and that the main products of the region would probably be wool and grain. Thereupon the French authorities gravely directed a number of buffaloes be penned up, tamed, shorn of their wool at the proper time, and be generally taught the ways of civilized cattle. Ah, those were quiet old times. Things have changed since then.

But did they tame the buffaloes?' innocently asked Bea, when I told the story; and I only laughed at the simplicity of her question. The idea of taming buffaloes and shearing their alleged wool! One would think an American girl would scarcely ask such a question.

I am forgetting the Biloxi of the present in the past, and I fancy those early Frenchmen would hardly recognize the place to-day. Bathing houses line the beach, there are splendid drives, and the town itself with its excellent hotels and accommodations for the stranger is inviting. Even religion has chosen its particular dwelling here, and the Methodists have a large park where camp meetings are annually held, and which is at all times a delightful pleasure ground. These meetings were very humble affairs at first, but year by year they grew and they are still growing. The great trees which line the shore at Biloxi cast a grateful shade, and on the benches beneath them one loves to linger and look out upon the Gulf. Not far off—about three miles—Deer Island can be seen. It is almost as level as the water which surrounds it, and it makes a pleasant run for a short sail. Further out on the Gulf are Cat and Ship Islands. On the latter there was a military prison during the war, and many confederates were kept there under the galling wardenship of colored troops. That was one of General Ben. F. Butler's savage practical jokes.

Fort Massachusetts was built on Ship Island, and it was a place of considerable strength, although to-day the tourist will find that it has almost disappeared. But there was a more famous fort within the town, Fort Biloxi, where French soldiers for many years kept guard, and under the shelter of its guns the hardy traders who not only ventured up and down the coast, but even ran across to Mexico, have often rested. The gay song of the light-hearted Canadian voyagers rang across the waters where now swells the solemn, glorious strains of the camp meeting hymns. No longer the sentinel tramps up and down the ramparts of the long deserted Fort watching for the Indian or the Spaniards, but merry children romp upon the beach in play, and men and women find health and strength in the breezes that come from the South and West. But still the country is very much as the French found it. The face of nature has been but little changed. The immediate neighborhood of Biloxi is the same as it was a thousand years ago, and the waves of the Gulf still sparkle in the sunshine, or are lashed in the storm as when the Children of Israel were toiling through the desert to the Promised Land. In other parts of America man has almost entirely altered the appearance of the land, but here the physical conditions forbid anything of the kind.

The road beyond Biloxi still skims along by the side of the Gulf, while the air is filled with the aroma of the pines which are green and beautiful the year around. The soil is very sandy yet the pine trees flourish, and a kind of long grass grows in great luxuriant tufts. Occasionally we catch a glimpse of the blue waters, now the train is dashing through the pines where there are long vistas between the trees, where the ground looks so soft and inviting that Bea, as on a former occasion, wishes that we could get out and take a stroll. It is through scenes like these that we pass until we reach Beauvoir.

"This is the home of Mr. Jefferson Davis, President of the late Southern Confederacy," observes the conductor.

"Can you see his house from the station?" asks Bea.

And she is quite disappointed to learn that the mansion is not visible. She half hopes that the distinguished gentleman will be waiting at the station to take the train for New Orleans, but he is not there to gratify her curiosity. Mr. Davis lives here on quite an extensive estate in a most quiet and unostentatious fashion. His days are passed in studious retirement and he sees little or no company.

Five miles beyond Beauvoir is Mississippi City, another charming place, and a resort of many attractions. Many people from New Orleans spend their summers here, and the long beach is an admirable place for bathing, while there is the best of fishing off it. Peace and quiet seem to brood over the town, and the houses with their massive white pillars are in themselves an invitation to rest and enjoyment. All around are the most delightful walks, and nature appears to have made the region especially for man's delectation.

Pass Christian and Bay St. Louis

These are the great places of resort for the New Orleanites. They are two beautiful towns which lie on either side of Bay St. Louis, and they are, to use a happy Biblical phrase, "altogether lovely." Pass Christian is the unique town of all unique towns. The man who called it Shostringville was very felicitous in his description. It stretches along the Gulf for six miles, and is but one house deep. Villas and cottages line the landward side of the hard, smooth, shell road which is the delight and pride of the residents, while in front of nearly all the houses a long narrow wharf stretched from the shore to deep water. As a rule these wharves end in either a boat or a bath house. Many of these villas are built with an eye to "style," while others were plainly constructed for "solid home comfort."

In the evening the shell road is fairly alive with vehicles, and this is the great event of the day among those who are summering or wintering at the Pass. And what a drive it is! The road is as hard as asphalt, and it is as smooth as a ball room floor. The horses actually find it a pleasure to put their "best foot foremost, and many are the good-natured races which take place, the drivers encouraged to bring out all the speed there is in their animals by the smiles of the beauties of the South. Happy and light are the hearts that beat at Pass Christian, and gay are the revels at the splendid Mexican Gulf Hotel. When the summer with its heavy heat lies drowsily upon New Orleans its people flock to this favored spot. This is a

"Delicious land of lavish lights and floating shades."

And when at even-tide the light fades out of the West and the waters of the Bay softly roll upon the sand, the dreamer can well imagine that this is a region of romance and the realities of the present go with the dying day, and he repeats:

> "Little breezes, dusk and shiver,
> This the wave that runs forever
> By the island in the river
>   Flowing down to Camelot.
> Four gray walls, and four gray towers,
> Overlook a space of flowers,
> And the silent isle embowers
>   The Lady of Shalott."

As the light of day goes out the lights in Bay St. Louis begin to twinkle across the water, and from the windows of the hotel there streams a flood of splendor. The town is very much like its neighbor. There

LAGOONS BY MOONLIGHT.

is a shell road, the same long narrow wharves and bathing houses, and the same beautiful summer residences half hidden by the luxuriant foliage. The Ellen N. cuts directly across the mouth of the Bay, on a long trestle. "We're taking a ride on the water," exclaimed Bea, as we crossed it.

And it looked very much like it. Looking out of the car windows water was to be seen on either hand, and we could not have more thoroughly felt that we were on the sea, "the glorious sea," if we had been taking a ride in an ocean steamer. But what a glorious view it was! Far away extended the blue Bay until shut in by sandy headlands crowned with pine. The waters of the Gulf sparkled in the sunshine, bright and beautiful. To the West lay Bay St. Louis with its white houses and pretty church forming a picturesque ensemble, while to the East lay Pass Christian. Sails dotted the horizon, and light pleasure yachts were darting in and out. He who has seen this scene in the glory of the sunshine can never forget it. Search where you will on the Atlantic Coast or on the shores of the Great Lakes, nowhere is there a spot so purely beautiful and so favored by bounteous nature as this.

The tourist bent on pleasure will doubtless be surprised to learn that Bay St. Louis is a place of some commercial importance. It possesses the only woollen mill on the coast, and carries on a trade in lumber of considerable extent. At the head of the Bay are a number of logging streams and the timber of course comes from them. Its population is between 2,500 and 3,000.

It is just fifty-two miles by the Ellen N. from Bay St. Louis to New Orleans, and a marvelous stretch of road it is. Joaquin Miller rode over it on a glorious afternoon in December, and was fired with its beauty and unique loveliness. Well he knew how to describe the region, when he wrote. "And we are dashing right against the sun as it falls into the sea. The Crescent City and the great river are fifty, forty, thirty miles away. Lagoons behind us, and bayous before us and right and left of us. Little clumps of oaks and ash and beech are springing up right and left from out the vast brown levels of marsh; and men hunt here for deer, thirty miles from the city, and shoot 'canvas backs' by the ship load.

"On, on in the face of the falling sun. The sun is in the sea. But there is a conflagration of earth and of air. The heavens are illuminated. They know we are coming. There is a scene of conquest, of discovery, as we come near this olden city by the great river, all in the face of the burning heavens. Ah, don't you know that if this sunset, this scene, this water and this land, this air and illumination were in Europe, the writers there—upheld, countenanced, encouraged by the country—would lift them up in glory so that all the world should be compelled to come and see?"

I read Bea what Joaquin Miller said, as we dashed on through the marshes and glimmering lagoons.

"Ah!" said she, "it takes a poet to put in words what one feels."

And as we pass over these vast swampy levels, through which the lazy bayous trace their way-like canals, we remark that if the landscape were but furnished with a wind-mill or two that it would be remarkably like Holland. The railroad here is a wonder of engineering skill. The swamp is almost fathomless; the black ooze everywhere being soft and yielding. For nearly thirty miles the track is either built upon ponderous piles, driven deep into the unsubstantial mire, or upon embankments of sand.

"It took a world of labor to make these embankments," said an old railroader to me; "and in some places they are actually boxed in to protect them from the slow sopping of the water."

Waveland, Toulme and Claiborne are successively passed, and at last we reach the Rigolets. The "Rigolets" is nothing else than a strait, or sluggish water way, connecting Lake Bargne, which is off the Gulf of Mexico, and Lake Ponchartrain. Steamers going from Mobile and along the coast reach the rear of New Orleans by this route. It is a queer spot, and it is hard to tell whether the land or water predominates. So level is the locality that the tall reeds hide the bayous that wind their devious ways in and out among them, and the boats that slowly move either toward New Orleans or the Gulf, seem to be gliding along the land. Lake Catharine is simply a station, where in the season, sportsmen come to shoot water fowl.

"This calls to mind," observed Bea, as she looked out upon the beautiful stretch of the Lake and then upon the land, which seemed to be more or less like the lake, "the poets 'water, water everywhere.'"

"And not a drop to drink," I added, "for it is horribly brackish."

Six miles further on is Chef Mentum, another water way to Lake Ponchartrain. It is only a stopping-place in the marsh and the passenger looks with curiosity upon the little custom house, built on piles and above which floats the revenue flag, with its bars running the wrong way, and an old-fashioned circular fort which the Ellen N. passes within a stone's throw. It is Fort Macomb, built long ago to defend the rear approaches to the Crescent City. But now no flag flutters from its flag-staff and no sunrise or sunset gun sets the echoes rolling. No garrison is needed there in "these piping times of peace," and so no officers or men are exiled to this dreary spot. Life in such a place with its unvarying routine must have been monotonous enough to have made the soldiers wish for the comparative liveliness of the tomb. And how much more inexpressibly solitary it must have been before the railroad cheered the spot with its presence.

It is not a great distance now to New Orleans, and the Ellen N. on this home stretch goes through a region as wild and tropical as in the most characteristic portions of Florida. Rugged, gnarled live oaks lift themselves from the half reclaimed swamp land and their every branch is draped with long gray Spanish Moss. Pines and Cypresses are hidden by this mysterious plant of the air, and it veils the nakedness of their limbs and kindly hides the ravages of time. The watery wastes are filled with palmettoes, whose green bayonet-like shafts gleam in the sunshine, while beneath them the lazy alligator slowly crawls away frightened by the thunder of the rushing train.

"Lor' bless you, miss," said the porter to Bea, "there's more 'gators in dis here swamp than dere's people in Norf America. When they all done built dis railroad de 'gators was so plenjous dat dey used them for railroad ties. Solemn truf! for de Lor', miss, for I'se seed 'em a thousand times."

And Bea smiles in very evident doubt. But now Lee, Micheand and Gentilly have been passed and houses begin to appear on the right and left. We are in the environs of New Orleans and the train slows up as it enters the city. On and on, however, past the strange looking houses and narrow streets, until at last the Mississippi, Father of Waters, bursts upon our eyes and we see the multitudinous vessels that lie at the far extended wharves, we catch a glimpse of the busy levee, and while all these new and unaccustomed sights are still bewildering us the train stops. Our journey for the present is over. We are in New Orleans and we find as we leave the car that Ellen N. has kindly brought us right into the heart of the city and landed us at the foot of Canal Street, the great central thoroughfare of the place.

New Orleans

"You'll find New Orleans just like a foreign city," said a lady at the hotel to Bea. "and you can see it without crossing the ocean and being dreadfully sea-sick." "And do you know what I told her?" observed my sister when she afterward quoted the remark to me. "No, what was it?" "Why, I said that riding on the Ellen N. to New Orleans and having a delightful time all the trip, was a great deal better than being sea-sick." But I must not wander away from the thread of my narrative to tell what we said, but what we saw. And we saw so much that really I hardly know where to begin. We found New Orleans to be, indeed, a foreign city and everything seemed very strange to our eyes, while the multitude of languages heard on the streets was enough to drive an ordinary man crazy. But it was all bewilderingly new and delightfully odd. Of course Bea and I were first taken with Canal street, which has unchanging charms for the stranger and resident alike. It is a great thoroughfare which runs directly through the city, its main artery in fact, from which branch off the other streets. Canal street is most tremendously wide. It is the widest street, I think, in America; in fact it is two streets with a strip of green sward between them. Once on a time that narrow bit of green was neutral ground. The French and Americans for some time did not get along together as peacefully as might be wished, and separate municipal governments were maintained. On the east side of Canal the French held sway, to the west was the American quarter, and the long, tree-shaded promenade in the middle of the wide street was no man's land. Just now, however, this neutral ground appears to have been pretty thoroughly monopolized by the street cars. Every line in New Orleans, and by the way visiting Bostonians, anxious to be minutely correct, call the cars "mule cars," starts on Canal street, and the cars always begin and finish their trip at the same place. There are little sentry boxes in the middle of the street at the crossings and Bea and I were not long in finding that the men who occupied them were as good as guide books. "Canal street," sagely remarked Bea, "improves upon acquaintance. I never saw such a street for shipping, and with the stores and windows all open so that you can see everything there is to sell. Then think of the people we have seen, Americans, half a dozen different kinds, Frenchmen, Germans, Mexicans, Spaniards, Italians, and I don't know how many others." And I guess that it is a good street for shopping, not to mention its splendid buildings and the magnificent effects produced by distance, for Bea dragged me into twenty stores where neither of us wanted to buy anything. I need hardly say that the first place which we set out to visit in earnest was the French Market. We had heard of it long before we had read George W. Cable's novels, still they had stirred our curiosity more than ever. To reach the market take a car on Canal street, or you can walk, as it is only about five squares from the Post Office. Were we disappointed? No, the half has never been told. Of course, the market buildings are more or less like all such structures, except for their great size, but the diversified multiplicity of what is offered for sale is without a precedent unless a score or two of Wandering Jews might get together, and forming a pool, start an auction. The buyers and sellers are a study.

"What in the world is there," I asked Bea, "that can not be bought here? I just saw a man selling kid gloves, and I've noticed that everything else that a man might want for his toilet, from a pair of shoes to a silk hat, is for sale."

"And I've noticed," she chimed in, "that a woman might dress herself from top to toe, while you can furnish a house attic to cellar, not to mention the fact that there is almost enough food in sight to keep an army for a week or two, and it includes all the 'delicacies of the season,' as the papers say."

And then the people! they furnish entertainment in themselves, and the most careless observer finds something of interest from the old Indian woman—at least they look old—who sell reed baskets and gumbo, and on and on up to the prettiest and most modern French girl selling bon-bons. Every visitor buys something as a souvenir, and of course invests in fruit. Oranges and bananas purchased at the French market have a peculiar tropical sweetness, and really one never knows the real deliciousness of Southern fruit until he goes South. Then, too, strangers must take a cup of *café au lait*, or *café noir* which, translated, means coffee with milk or black coffee. Bea said that the *café au lait* was about as bad as the coffee that our last new cook made, or rather tried to make; but I found mine extremely palatable, while it was jolly fun to sit at one of the market tables and eat the fresh bayou oysters.

Just opposite the market is Jackson Square and the Cathedral. In the center of the square is a statue of "Old Hickory," identical with the one we had already seen at Nashville. The square is a very pretty Park, filled with blooming tropical plants and shrubbery; while orange trees, yellow with fruit, shade the benches. Small, white shells form the paths which circle about the square; and Bea was greatly taken with the children who romped around, chatting away in French, and occasionally breaking out in English.

"They play just like our Cincinnati children," remarked Bea, as though she had made an unlooked-for discovery.

Then I went on to explain that of course they did, for Americans are Americans the world over; and, my explanation finished, we strolled over to the Cathedral. It is a very old stuccoed structure, built in a semi-Spanish-Mexican style, and it shows its age. We entered by the little side door, for the ponderous front doors are only opened on feast days and Sundays, and were startled by the beauty of the interior. Here is some of the finest frescoeing and mural painting to be found on the continent. There is one especially fine piece back of the high altar. It is a picture of St. Louis; the good and gentle Louis IX. starting out on his last crusade. He is dressed in the garb of the Crusader, with the holy red cross upon his breast, his Queen stands by his side, while the nobles of his gorgeous Court and a brilliant array of Cardinals and prelates are ranged around. Then the pictures of the Apostles, heroic size, are most excellent.

There was another church which we visited, and which the stranger should not miss seeing. It is the Church of the Jesuits on Baronne street, just a square from Canal; and its elaborate interior decorations remind one of some of the splendidly ornamented halls in the Alhambra.

But to return to the Cathedral. On either side is a characteristically Spanish building, whose heavy pillared arcades are unique. They are used as Court Houses, and it seems very odd to see modern, nineteenth century notices of law-suits stuck over their ancient, seventeenth century sides.

Of course we rambled over the French part of the city and saw its beauties a-foot. All visitors see the French quarter on foot—that is, if they see it at all—for riding is simply an aggravation; then, beside, very few of the streets are wide enough to ride through, anyhow.

"These houses are a never-ending surprise," said Bea, after one of these long rambles. "There are no duplicates, and each house seems to have been built on a plan of its own."

I need not say that the result has been peculiar. The houses in New Orleans admit of everything; but one thing they must have, and that is, plenty of verandas. One veranda will not answer—there must be verandas on verandas and shaded balconies on shaded balconies. But, if the visitor is not wary, he will find that the charming bric-a-brac stores in the French quarter will utterly drain his pocket-book; but, at the same time, the French restaurants will fill his stomach and make life seem worth the living. The restaurants are intensely New Orleanish. They are not only one of the institutions, but one of the curiosities. You are served a delicious dinner—the cooking being thoroughly and delightfully French—for fifty cents, and a small bottle of light wine comes with it. Dinner is not eaten until late in the afternoon, for here people sensibly eat their heavy meal at their leisure, after the day's work is done, and the evening is given up to social amusement.

Bea had somehow formed the idea that Lake Pontchartrain was a big, muddy pond, and she was very much surprised on visiting it to find an inland lake, whose waters stretched away until the sky closed down upon them. There are two places on the Lake which are to be seen, West End and Spanish Fort. To reach them take the dummy, or narrow gauge railway, that starts on Canal street above Carondelet. The fare is only fifteen cents. These two resorts are the Coney Island and Rockaway Beach of New Orleans. Here are magnificent gardens, rare trees, broad pavilions, great hotels; and in the sultry nights of summer the people throng here by the thousands. They listen to the music, see a comic opera or comedy, promenade through the grounds or gather at the tables and talk over their cream and lemonade, or it is perhaps something stronger. We found the ride to the lake very charming. The roads lead directly through the swamps which environ New Orleans; and its distinctively tropical vegetation was grateful to our Northern eyes. On the return-trip from West End stop-off, at the cemeteries, it will cost nothing extra — and take a stroll through them. It is hard to say whether the old or new cemetery is the most interesting. Of course everybody knows the dead are buried in tombs above the ground; for if graves were dug they would be filled with water even as the spade went down into the earth. Some of the tombs are more than a century old, and the epitaphs in French, you know, breathe a spirit of simple piety that is beautiful. The tombs and monuments in the new cemetery are more pretentious than those which were built earlier, and are more in keeping with modern ideas. We especially noted the tomb of General Albert Sidney Johnson — that brave Southern soldier, who fell fighting at the awful battle of Shiloh — and the monuments to General Robert E. Lee and the Confederate dead. Many of these tombs are built like miniature Grecian temples. Others follow the lighter Gothic style of architecture; while again others have been built according to the uncurbed fancy of the architect. "I don't want to be sacreligious," observed Bea, as we passed beneath an orange tree in the new cemetery; "but some of these tombs are just fitted for the Romeo and Juliet story." You see that a young girl's fancy lightly turns to thoughts of love tales even amid the most solemn surroundings; and the environments of these cemeteries are most certainly solemnly mournful. All around the gloomy swamp shuts them in, while the tall cedars and live oaks, heavy with drooping Spanish moss, close the vista. These bare trees are inexpressibly sad. Many are dead; yet the moss, which has sucked the sap of their life, still lives

MAGNOLIAS.

BEA'S MARDI-GRAS.

and flourishes. Where could a better emblem be found of that specter of which Coleridge speaks, Life in Death? And now we take the cars, and, riding past beautiful residences and wide extended gardens — themselves worth a visit, we are again amid the hum and bustle of Canal street. On Mardi-Gras and Christmas Eve this great thoroughfare, always interesting and attractive, is at its best. It is then superlative. Christmas Eve is observed by a grand imitation, or rather realistic representation, of Pandemonium. Bea keeps a diary, and I remember that she graciously read me some extracts, one of which ran as follows: "'Tis the night before Christmas, and all of the boys are blowing tin horns and making a noise." Noise is a mild term — infernal racket would be better. Northern people think Fourth of July is bad enough, but it does not begin to compare with Christmas Eve in New Orleans. All the city throngs Canal street, and everybody that is not blowing a tin horn is firing off Chinese crackers or fire-works of some kind. Overhead, the long row of electric light twinkle and blaze; and below, the wide avenue seems on fire. All is light and movement; everybody is joyously laughing. Even the preternaturally solemn mules of the street cars grow frisky and sportive, and fling up their heels in a highly suggestive manner. On Christmas Eve all New Orleans is bent on having a good time and making a noise; and they succeed. But when Mardi-Gras comes the city is yet madder and merrier. Flags and gay banners flutter from all the houses, and when night comes the Carnival is wildly joyous. Then comes the gorgeous procession of the Mystic Krewe, which presents one of the most brilliant spectacles in the world. I feel, however, that it is almost a waste of time and paper to speak of the Carnival; for where is there a traveler who has not read all about it a hundred times? At the foot of Canal street, and just beyond the L. & N. Depot, is the levee, where is piled the merchandise of an extensive and ever-growing trade. There are bales and bales of cotton, hundreds of barrels of sugar, and hogsheads of molasses without number; while there are enough roustabouts, all singing their strange songs, to people a colony. The great ocean steamers lie side by side with the "floating palaces" that ply up and down the Mississippi. Perhaps a man-of-war lies in mid-channel, with her bow sturdily pointed up stream, while the flag of her nation floats from the peak. Across the river lie the towns of Algiers and Tunis. The river makes a grand sweep as it flows toward the Gulf beyond the city, and this is called the "English Turn." In the war of 1812 the English sailed up to this point, but they never went further. Gen. Jackson stopped them, and the old battle-ground is still to be seen. In the late war the batteries of Chalmette were planted on the spot, and hard by is the Great National Cemetery, where hundreds of the "boys in blue" lie awaiting the bugle-blast which will summon them to "fall in" the Eternal Ranks. Here is the G. A. R. monument, and the visitor will find it worth seeing. Walking down the levee as far as Esplanade street, the U. S. Mint is reached, the Sugar Exchange having been passed on the way.

Bea and I not only took the customary trip to the "jetties," which are really very interesting—although the ride on the river and the views *en passant* are by far the best part of the journey—but we took a ride up the river and visited several sugar plantations. A good plan is to go up the river as far as Baton Rouge, and then come back. The tourist obtains in this way an excellent idea of the country, sees the levees, the bayous, and learns more about Louisiana along the river than he could if he read a thousand books.

Once again in New Orleans, we rambled again over the streets, now grown familiar, but none the less attractive. Again we visited the gloomy post-office, dark and heavy externally, with its Egyptian exterior, but with a great hall, which quite redeems the structure. This hall is of white marble, and at one end is a very handsome piece of mural sculpture. There is the pelican nursing her young, the seal of Louisiana; and on one side is Bienville, founder of New Orleans—and on the other Jackson, its defender. Again we took long rides through the residence streets; and in fact the city is more or less a huge suburb. Once more we delighted in the oddities of the French quarter, and reveled in the deliciousness of the fruit purchased in the French market. Then we packed up our traps and prepared to take a run through Florida. But I must say a word about the hotels. The tourist will find that in New Orleans he can secure first-class accommodations at just what he would pay in other American cities. And, if he wishes, he can secure rooms and eat where he pleases; for the restaurants are not only numerous, but exceptionally good.

If the traveler is going further West, he can slip over to Galveston, Texas, and from thence on through the Lone Star State to Mexico.

W. N. HALDEMAN,
PRESIDENT.

SUNDAY
DAILY
WEEKLY.

HENRY WATTERSON,
EDITOR.

THE LOUISVILLE COURIER-JOURNAL,

THE REPRESENTATIVE NEWSPAPER OF THE SOUTH,

Its Weekly Issue having the Largest Circulation of any Democratic Newspaper in the United States.

THE COURIER-JOURNAL has a national reputation; it is the acknowledged Representative Newspaper of the South; is Democratic in Politics; and, first, last, and all the time, is for a Reduction of the War Taxes, as levied on the people by the tariff now in force.

The Daily and Sunday editions of the COURIER-JOURNAL are not only recognized as the direct representatives of a vast majority of the newspaper readers in Louisville and in the State of Kentucky, but also have a wide circulation throughout the South and West.

THE WEEKLY COURIER-JOURNAL is the best weekly newspaper published in the United States, and for the quantity and quality of matter that appears in each issue of it, it is the Cheapest. Its Telegraphic News facilities outclass any other paper, and it has the services of the ablest writers and correspondents in the country. It presents the News of the Week from every section of the world. It gives to its readers, throughout the year, a greater number of Serial and Short Stories by prominent and popular writers than any of the high-priced magazines. It is in every respect a Model Political and Family Paper.

THE WEEKLY COURIER-JOURNAL HAS BY FAR THE LARGEST CIRCULATION OF ANY DEMOCRATIC NEWSPAPER IN AMERICA.

THE WEEKLY COURIER-JOURNAL has no rival in the South. The Southern people recognize it as being in full sympathy with their social life, and as the ablest and truest exponent of their political convictions. Its circulation among farmers is equal to that of any exclusive agricultural weekly. Into their homes it is warmly welcomed as a friend, and we say with confidence that satisfactory returns are certain from any investment in its advertising columns. Its circulation in some of the Southern States is equal to that of the combined circulation of all the newspapers of those States. It is acknowledged by press and people throughout the United States to be a great paper—great in size, great in enterprise, great in ability, great in its correctness of information, great in variety, great in every sense of the word. It is the paper that everybody should have.

There are but few post-offices in all the South that it does not go to every week in the year. It is not only creditable to the enterprise of its publishers, but equally a credit to the city of Louisville, where it is published, that the WEEKLY COURIER-JOURNAL should have attained the enormous circulation our subscription lists show it to have. It regularly visits each week in the year over 100,000 homes—the homes of its yearly subscribers and, as each copy sent out has at least four or five readers, it regularly reaches over half a million readers.

FREE PREMIUMS. A list of handsome and useful premiums, of great variety, are offered to our yearly subscribers. On receipt of a request for them, we will send, free of charge, a sample copy of WEEKLY COURIER-JOURNAL and our Premium Supplement, giving our full list of premiums, free, without any addition.

SUBSCRIPTION TERMS.

Weekly, one year, without premium,	$1.25
Weekly, one year, including a free premium,	1.50
Weekly, to clubs of five and over, without premium, each,	1.10
Weekly, to clubs of five and over, with free premium to each subscriber, each,	1.30

For every Club of Five Names sent us at one time, the sender of Club will be sent, as a present, any one of our Free Premiums, selected by him.

Daily (except Sunday), one year,	10.00
Daily (except Sunday), six months,	5.00
Daily (except Sunday), one month,	.90
Sunday, one year, $2.00 Sunday, six months,	1.00

No Traveling Agents are employed by the COURIER-JOURNAL, but a good Local Agent is wanted for it in every community, to whom a liberal cash commission is allowed. If the COURIER-JOURNAL has no Local Agent in your neighborhood, send to us for our Agent's Canvassing Outfit, which we send free of charge.

All advertisements, subscription orders, requests for outfits, sample copies, etc., should be addressed to

W. N. HALDEMAN,   LOUISVILLE, KY.

Ohio Falls Car Company,

JEFFERSONVILLE, IND.

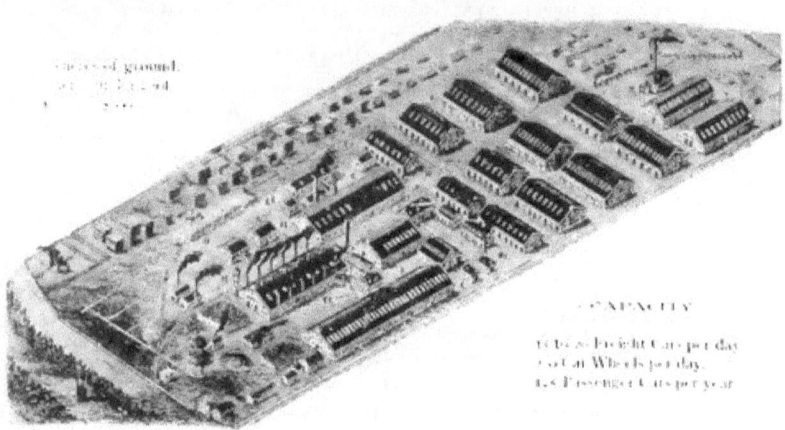

· BUILDER AND MANUFACTURER ·

of

PASSENGER AND FREIGHT

· Railroad Cars · ·

· · Car Wheels · ·

CAR AND OTHER CASTINGS,

BRASSES AND FORGINGS

Our facilities for obtaining materials — Coal, Iron and Lumber —, both by river and rail, are unsurpassed by any other Car Works in the United States.

DR. JOHN BULL'S
SMITH'S · TONIC · SYRUP

FOR THE CURE OF

FEVER AND AGUE, OR CHILLS AND FEVER,

AND ALL MALARIAL DISEASES.

THE proprietor of this celebrated medicine justly claims for it a superiority over all remedies ever offered to the public for the *safe, certain, speedy* and *permanent* cure of Ague and Fever, or Chills and Fever, whether of short or long standing. He refers to the entire western and southern country to bear him testimony to the truth of the assertion that in no case whatever will it fail to cure if the directions are strictly followed and carried out. In a great many cases a single dose has been sufficient for a cure, and whole families have been cured by a single bottle, with a perfect restoration of the general health. It is, however, prudent and in every case more certain to cure, if its use is continued in smaller doses for a week or two after the disease has been checked, more especially in difficult and long-standing cases. Usually this medicine will not require any aid to keep the bowels in good order. Should the patient, however, require a cathartic medicine, after having taken three or four doses of the Tonic, a single dose of KENT'S VEGETABLE FAMILY PILLS will be sufficient. ☞ USE NO OTHER PILLS.

BULL'S SARSAPARILLA is the old and reliable remedy for impurities of the blood and scrofulous affections—the King of Blood Purifiers.

BULL'S VEGETABLE WORM DESTROYER is prepared in the form of Candy Drops, attractive to the sight and pleasant to the taste.

DR · JOHN · BULL'S

SMITH'S TONIC SYRUP,
BULL'S SARSAPARILLA,
BULL'S WORM DESTROYER.

The Popular Remedies of the Day.

Principal Office,   LOUISVILLE, KY.   831 West Main St

⋮ MAGNOLIA ☆ HAM ⋮

FROM A CURE
OF
7,000 PIECES
IN 1873,
THE
MAGNOLIA
HAS ATTAINED
AN
ANNUAL CURE
OF
375,000

WE EXPECT
TO
EXTEND
THE CURE
OF THE
MAGNOLIA
TO
500,000
PIECES.

The Magnolia is the Largest Cure of strictly Winter Sugar-Cured Canvased Hams made in the World

THE MOST DELICIOUS HAMS. THE MAGNOLIA IS CURED UNDER THE BEST FORMULA KNOWN, WITH THE FINEST AND MOST EXPENSIVE INGREDIENTS. THE ART OF HAM-CURING HAS CULMINATED IN THE MAGNOLIA. THE PROOF OF THE PUDDING IS IN THE EATING.

Ask Your Grocer for MAGNOLIAS And Take No Other

☞ EVERY HAM GUARANTEED. ☜

SPRING HILL DISTILLERY
· HAND-MADE · SOUR MASH WHISKY.

THE "SPRING HILL" WHISKY is the product of a distillery located near Frankfort, Franklin County, the Capital of Kentucky, and is situated at a point immediately between L. C. & L. Railroad and the Kentucky River. Shipments are made by either, without cartage. This location is in the finest Whisky-producing district of the State, which is the home of all the most expensive and popular brands of the State. The "SPRING HILL" has no superior among them all, and we have every confidence that a trial with any of them will result in such a conclusion.

IT is rich and full in flavor, without the coarseness characteristic of so much of the Kentucky Whisky. With age it takes on the flavor of Madeira Wine or a fine Cognac Brandy. We own some of the Whisky of each year's production up to this time, which has never been out of our possession. That which is obtained from us may be relied upon for absolute purity and of the age it is represented to be. Whether for the connoisseur or the invalid we unhesitatingly recommend it. The picture accompanying this advertisement is a fac-simile representation of the Distillery premises.

IN order that persons, who desire to secure Whisky, good and in every way reliable, in small quantity, we put up the oldest six years, in cases of one dozen bottles each. The labels have a similar representation of the Distillery.

FOR the reliability of our statements we refer to the Bankers, Merchants, Physicians and the citizens generally of Louisville and Frankfort, Ky.

· · ·

JNO. COCHRAN & CO.
PROPRIETORS.
FRANKFORT, KY.

THE COCHRAN FULTON CO.
GEN'L AGENTS
LOUISVILLE, KY.

Chess-Carley Company, LOUISVILLE, KY.

· Illuminating Oil. · Lubricating Oil. ·

SPECIALTY ✦ FIRE-PROOF OIL

ABSOLUTE SAFETY FOR SOUTHERN HOMES.

GOLD MEDAL AWARDED
BY THE
World's Industrial Exposition, New Orleans.

BRANCHES

Albany, Ga.
Atlanta, Ga.
Augusta, Ga.
Birmingham, Ala.
Brunswick, Ga.
Cairo, Ills.
Charleston, S. C.
Charlotte, N. C.
Chattanooga, Tenn.
Chicago, Ills.
Columbia, S. C.
Columbus, Ga.
Helena, Ark.
Henderson, Ky.
Jacksonville, Fla.

BRANCHES

Lexington, Ky.
Ludlow, Ky.
Lumber City, Ga.
Macon, Ga.
Mobile, Ala.
Memphis, Tenn.
Meridian, Miss.
Nashville, Tenn.
New Orleans, La.
Owensboro, Ky.
Paducah, Ky.
Pensacola, Fla.
Savannah, Ga.
Vicksburg, Miss.
Wilmington, N. C.

GOLD MEDAL AWARDED
BY THE
Southern Exposition,
LOUISVILLE, KY.

TURPENTINE · ROSIN ·

WRAMPELMEIER & CO.

MANUFACTURERS

WHOLESALE AND
RETAIL DEALERS
IN ALL KINDS OF

FURNITURE, MATTRESSES, ETC.

CHAMBER,
DRAWING ROOM,
PARLOR,

FURNITURE

LIBRARY,
DINING ROOM,
OFFICE,

HOTEL,
PUBLIC HALL,
LODGE,

UPHOLSTERY

SOCIETY,
CHURCH,
BANK, Etc.

STORES: — 544, 546, 548 & 550 Fourth Ave.   FACTORY   Fifteenth, Rowan and Portland Ave.

LOUISVILLE, KY.

CORNWALL & BROTHER.

LOUISVILLE, KY.

FINE MILLED TOILET AND LAUNDRY

· Soaps and Candles ·

Special Prices on Application

ESTABLISHED 1830

BRIDGEFORD & CO.

MANUFACTURERS OF

AMERICAN HOTEL, RESTAURANT, and FAMILY **RANGES**

ALSO SOLE MANUFACTURERS OF THE

ROYAL AMERICAN WOOD AND COLUMBIAN COAL
COOKING STOVES

FRANKLIN · ORIENT

Heating and Cooking Stoves.

LOUISVILLE, KY.   Send for Catalogue.   BRIDGEFORD & CO.

W. P. PYNE,

MACHINIST, MILLWRIGHT AND MILL FURNISHER.

MANUFACTURER OF

Portable · Corn · and · Wheat · Mills,

AND

MILL MACHINERY.

ALSO, BUILDER OF

STONE AND ROLLER MILLS

OF LATEST STYLES

Special Attention given to Grinding and Corrugating Rolls.

CONSTANTLY ON HAND FULL LINES OF

HOSE, BELTING, PACKING, BRASS GOODS, PIPE AND PIPE FITTINGS,

AND

MANUFACTURERS' SUPPLIES

JOBBING AND REPAIRING SOLICITED

AGENT FOR THE CELEBRATED

EUREKA WIND MILLS AND PUMPS

FOR SUPPLYING STOCK WATER

1107 West Main Street, LOUISVILLE, KY.

BARBEE & CASTLEMAN.

Fire · Insurance · Managers,

504 Main Street, Louisville, Ky

CONTROL
OVER
$40,000,000
OF
Fire Capital.

Adjust
and
Pay Their Own
Losses.

Managers of the

ROYAL · INSURANCE · COMPANY

and the

London · Lancashire · Fire · Insurance · Company,

of Liverpool.

Agents Throughout the South

✸ Dry·Goods ✸

CARTER BROTHERS & CO.

Importers and Jobbers.

729, 731, 733 West Main Street,

LOUISVILLE, KY.

NEW YORK OFFICE,
115 Worth Street.

·Notions and·Furnishing·Goods·

· Louisville Hotel ·

MAIN STREET, LOUISVILLE, KY.

The Chicago

Car Seal Co.

OFFICE:

Rooms 3, Quincy Building, **CHICAGO, ILLS.** No. 113 Adams Street.

MAKE AN EXCLUSIVE SPECIALTY OF MANUFACTURING

<u>Car Seals</u>,

<u>Sealing Punches</u>

<u>and Presses</u>,

<u>Car Door Seal Locks</u>

<u>and Fasteners</u>,

AND EVERYTHING PERTAINING TO THE CAR SEALING BUSINESS.

WE HAVE EXTENSIVE FACILITIES, AND CAN OFFER SPECIAL INDUCEMENTS BY PROMPTNESS AND LOW PRICES. SAMPLES AND MODELS SENT, AND PRICES GIVEN ON APPLICATION

WE SOLICIT YOUR BUSINESS, AND WILL BE PLEASED TO FURNISH ANY DESIRED INFORMATION.

WM. S. BREWSTER,
PRESIDENT

A. H. PEIRCE,
SEC'Y & TREAS.

ESTABLISHED 1839

✴ Brinly, ✴
Miles
AND
Hardy Co.

(Incorporated 1879.)

SOLE MANUFACTURERS

Main & Preston Sts.,

LOUISVILLE, KY

Nearly half a century of the most faithful and successful service in the field has shown the

Brinly Plow

to be, of all plows, the most durable, the simplest in mechanism, the lightest of draught, the most thorough in work, doing its work the most easily and steadily, the most readily adapted to all kinds of work, and the most easily renewed when worn.

BRINLY ONE-HORSE UNIVERSAL PLOW AND EXTRAS.

These striking and invaluable peculiarities justify its claim to be the BEST AND CHEAPEST PLOW in use, and have secured for it, after the most careful trial in the field, the unequaled number of

Over Seven Hundred Premiums,

Including those of the Great Southern Exposition, Louisville, etc., at which there was the largest display of Agricultural Implements ever made in the United States.

Only the highest attainable excellence in material, workmanship and performance will satisfy the Company, and that gives the farmer assurance of having always, when he buys a Brinly Plow, the best that can be made.

BRINLY TWO-HORSE UNIVERSAL PLOW

SEND FOR ILLUSTRATED CATALOGUE AND PRICE LIST TO   BRINLY, MILES & HARDY CO.   LOUISVILLE, KY.

LOW AND HIGH PRESSURE
Steam Warming and
Ventilating Apparatus,

SIMPLIFIED AND ADAPTED TO WARMING

ALL KINDS OF

PUBLIC AND PRIVATE BUILDINGS, RESIDENCES, CHURCHES, DEPOTS, Etc.

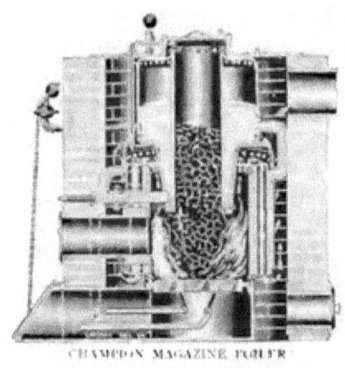

CHAMPION MAGAZINE BOILER

HOT WATER APPARATUS FOR GREEN HOUSES, Etc.

BAKER PATENT CAR WARMER

Baker, Smith & Co.

81 & 83 Jackson Street,   CHICAGO, ILLS.

→ Grand · Hotel ←

Opp. Grand Central Depot.   Cor. Fourth & Central Ave.

CINCINNATI, O.

RATES $3.00 and $4.00 per Day

ROOMS WITH BATHS AND PARLORS EXTRA

WHAT COMES FROM ONE PINT OF TROPIC CYLINDER OIL

On a leading Railroad during the month of September last, twenty round trips were made by alternating engineers on each locomotive. The result is,

7480 MILES FROM 91 PINTS, or 82⅕ MILES PER PINT OF TROPIC CYLINDER OIL, besides oiling Rod Bearings and Air Brakes.

During the month of October last, engines on the same Road, running in same way, made

5680 MILES FROM 60 PINTS, or 94⅔ MILES PER PINT OF TROPIC CYLINDER OIL, besides oiling six or eight Rod Bearings and usual Air Brakes.

On a different division of the same Road, engines operated in the same manner, made

2260 MILES FROM 25 PINTS, or 90⅖ MILES PER PINT OF TROPIC CYLINDER OIL, besides oiling Rod Bearings and Air Brakes.

The general average of mileage from our oil, for these two months, in all service, is not far from 62 miles per pint, and we are certain, with exceptionally favorable devices for feeding the oil, all these figures could have been greatly increased; but what we desire to show is actual average results. We want the benefit of the facts only.

Sample lots will be cheerfully sent to any Railroad desiring it, and we are certain of convincing even the most skeptical that, as to valve lubricants,

TROPIC CYLINDER OIL IS "BEST VALUE."

Respectfully,

CINCINNATI and ST. LOUIS. **INLAND OIL COMPANY.**

NEVER A DISTRESSED JOURNAL FROM POLAR GREASE,

IF YOU WILL PROVIDE AND USE AS **FOLLOWS THREE PACKERS' TUBS:**

FIRST—Put Waste and pour on just enough car oil to wet the fibre of the waste through and through. It is better to let stand and thoroughly soak for awhile.

SECOND—Put Oil and Polar Grease and mix together to the consistency of batter.

THIRD—Put the contents of tub No. 1 and No. 2 together and the Waste thoroughly saturated with the mixture. Your packing is now ready for the packer's use.

Journals dressed with this rich, fatty packing, run for weeks with but the least attention, rarely heat, and net a large mileage for a comparatively trifling cost.

MORE THAN HALF the trouble with journals arises from carelessly packing them. Every experienced Car Inspector knows this. By the plan herein shown

THE WASTE IS MADE MORE ELASTIC, and holds better up to journal.

THE OIL CHEAPENS THE FIRST COST of the Lubricant, and distributes it over the surfaces to greater advantage.

THE GREASE SUPPLIES BODY AND ACTUAL LUBRICATING POWER to the oils, which are too thin and lean in anti-friction for the Fast Passenger or heavily loaded Freight Trains of this day.

IN A WORD, the economy, the efficiency, and the lasting qualities of this Lubricating Compound are beyond comparison the best obtainable.

THESE ARE WORDS OF SOBER TRUTH. We have numerous letters from managers of leading railways, certifying to the success they have had with our Polar Grease, used

First.—FOR HOT BOX CURE.

Second.—FOR HOT BOX PREVENTIVE.

☛ Used as above stated, we guarantee satisfaction or no bills payable.

ORDERS SOLICITED.

INLAND OIL COMPANY, CINCINNATI AND ST. LOUIS.

❖HALL❖
Duplex ❖ Steam ❖ Pumps

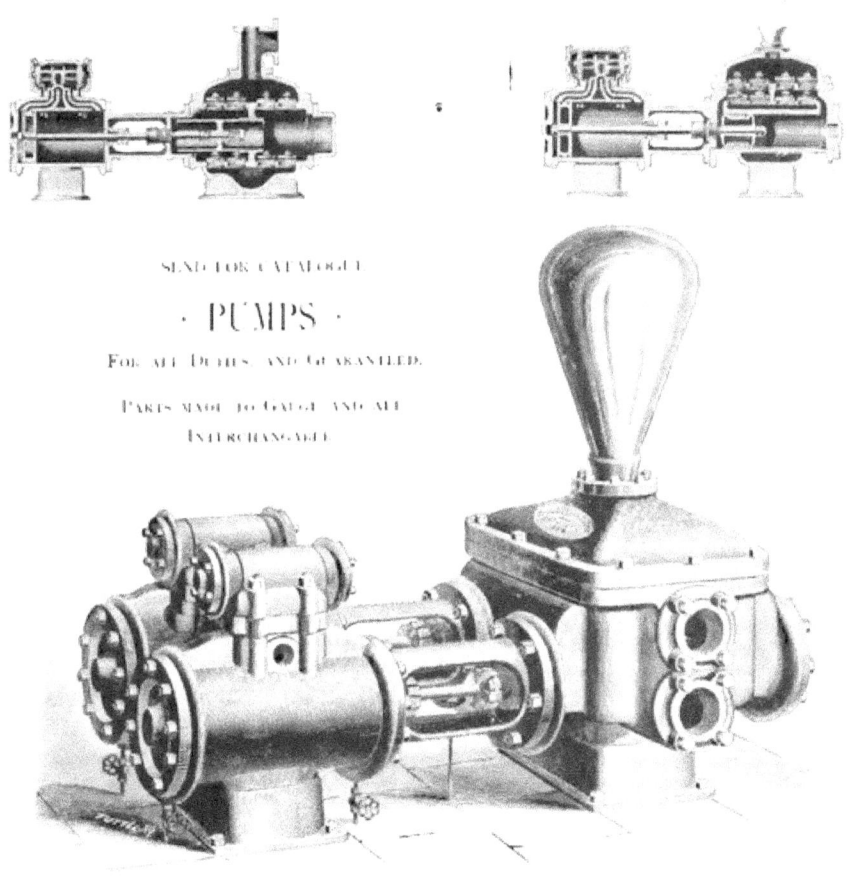

SEND FOR CATALOGUE

· PUMPS ·

FOR ALL DUTIES, AND GUARANTEED.

PARTS MADE TO GAUGE AND ALL
INTERCHANGEABLE.

FOR COMPACTNESS, SIMPLICITY, QUIETNESS, RELIABILITY AND DURABILITY
THESE PUMPS HAVE NO EQUAL.

HALL STEAM PUMP COMPANY

91 Liberty Street,   NEW YORK.

A. S. WHITON,

115 Broadway, - - New York.

Steel Rails, and
Rail Fastenings,
Steel Blooms, and
Steel Rail Crops.

✹ Railway ✹ Equipments ✹

Portland Cement and Block Chalk,

Old Rails and Railway Supplies,

Turntables and Rail Crossings.

Contracts made for delivery in the United States, West Indies, South America or F. O. B. English Ports.

Sole Agent in the United States for

The Northfleet Coal & Ballast Company,
Limited, of London.

CAST-STEEL-WORKS
OF
FRIED, KRUPP, ESSEN, GERMANY,

American Office, 15 Gold Street, New York.

REPRESENTED BY

THOS. PROSSER & SON,
P. O. Box 2878.

LOCOMOTIVE TIRES,

    AXLES, CRANK PINS,

        PISTON AND COUPLING RODS,

            SPRING AND TOOL STEEL.

STEEL FORGINGS, UP TO FIFTY TONS

        STEEL OF EVERY DESCRIPTION, FORGED, ROLLED, Etc.

            INTO ANY FORM OR ARTICLE DESIRED.

✺ STEEL-TIRED·WHEELS ✺

These Works cover an area of 1,200 acres, employ about 18,000 men, have the most improved plant and stand unique. They have their own Ore and Coal Mines, Blast Furnaces, etc., and EVERY stage of manufacture is under their own supervision, and they are not (like others) dependent on the open market for a miscellaneous assortment of crude material. This, in connection with seventy-five years' experience, enables them to turn out a product of very superior quality, second to none, and at the same time the different grades of Steel are always of the SAME UNIFORM QUALITY.

We beg to call special attention to KRUPP'S CRUCIBLE STEEL LOCOMOTIVE TIRES, which for the last thirty years have proved themselves to be the BEST and CHEAPEST in the market.

While the first cost of these is greater than of Open Hearth Steel (the grade usually furnished by other makers), it has been fully demonstrated that the extra amount invested in Krupp's Crucible Steel Tires, is more than refunded by the increased wear obtained from them, to say nothing of their freedom from breakage, and the saving effected in shop account, etc., by extra length of time Engines can be run before requiring Tires turned.

We call attention to the superior quality of Krupp's Axles, Crank Pins, Piston Rods, etc., which are being used by several of the leading Railways with most satisfactory results.

Being in daily cable communication with Works, we fill orders at short notice.

When ordering rolling stock, inserting in specifications that "Krupp's" Tires, Wheels (adding style of Wheel, with thickness, width and quality of Tire), Axles, etc., are to be used, will insure satisfactory articles.

ESTABLISHED 1827

Joseph Dixon Crucible Co.

JERSEY CITY, N.J.

MINERS, IMPORTERS, AND MANUFACTURERS OF

- GRAPHITE
- PLUMBAGO
- BLACK LEAD

- PENCILS
- CRUCIBLES
- STOVE POLISH

MAKERS OF THE CELEBRATED

• DIXON'S AMERICAN GRAPHITE PENCILS •

UNRIVALED for smoothness and toughness of Leads, freedom from grit, and uniformity of grades.—10 grades of hardness for Artists and Draughtsmen—7 grades for Office and School use, and over 500 other kinds in No. 2 and 3 leads for general use.

ALSO MANUFACTURERS OF

• DIXON'S CARBURET OF IRON STOVE POLISH •

THE oldest, best, and most reliable Stove Polish in the market. No dirt, no smell, and the quickest to produce a lasting polish.

• DIXON'S PURE DRY AMERICAN GRAPHITE •

ITS superiority as a lubricant has been attested by all recent writers on friction. Its enduring qualities are several times greater than those of any oil. Unlike either oil or grease it is not affected by either heat or cold, steam or acids. It is equally useful for metal or wood surfaces.

• DIXON'S PLUMBAGO CRUCIBLES •

ARE the standard in this country and in Europe. All sizes from ½ lb. to 600 lb. capacity.

• DIXON'S RAILWAY CAR GREASE •

Is unsurpassed for hot boxes and general lubricating purposes for railroads.

☞ *We shall be pleased to answer any and all inquiries concerning our products and to send explanatory circulars.*

The Louisville & Nashville R. R. use the Dixon Products.

(In writing please say you saw this Ad. in the L. & N. Book.)

The United States Rolling Stock Co.

OFFERS FOR

Lease to Railroads,
Freight Lines,
Mining Companies,
Locomotive Engines,
And Others,
Refrigerator Cars,
Box, Stock, Gondola,
Dump and Flat Cars.

Is prepared to build for lease and on contract for cash, or under the car trust system, such rolling stock as may be required.

CAPACITY OF SHOPS:

NEW WORKS AT HEGEWISCH,
Near Chicago, Ill.
Twenty Cars per Day.

AT URBANA, OHIO.
Sixteen Cars per Day.

STORAGE YARDS: Hegewisch, Ills., Urbana, O.

GENERAL OFFICES,
65 Wall St., New York.

A. HEGEWISCH, Pres't.

CHICAGO OFFICE,
180 La Salle Street

MANN · BOUDOIR · CAR

COMFORT!   PRIVACY!   LUXURY!
PERFECT VENTILATION!   NO DUST!   NO NOISE!

These Magnificent Cars are now running on the following Roads:

Cincinnati, New Orleans & Texas Pacific Railway, (Queen & Crescent)
CINCINNATI AND NEW ORLEANS.

Leave Cincinnati 7:10 A. M., 8:47 P. M.   Leave New Orleans 12:30 P. M., 8:55 P. M.

Louisville & Nashville and Queen & Crescent Roads.
LOUISVILLE AND CHATTANOOGA.

Leave Louisville 9:05 P. M.   Leave Chattanooga 6:28 P. M.

Georgia Pacific and Queen & Crescent.
ATLANTA AND NEW ORLEANS.

Leave Atlanta 4:30 P. M.   Leave New Orleans 12:30 P. M.

Queen & Crescent, E. T. V. & G., and S. F. & W. Railways.
CINCINNATI AND JACKSONVILLE, FLA.

Leave Cincinnati 7:40 A. M., 8:47 P. M.   Leave Jacksonville 7:30 A. M., 7:00 P. M.

Queen & Crescent, W. & A., and Central of Georgia Roads.
CINCINNATI AND JACKSONVILLE, FLA.

Leave Cincinnati 8:47 P. M.   Leave Jacksonville 7:00 P. M.

Wabash, St. Louis & Pacific Railway.
CHICAGO AND ST. LOUIS
CHICAGO AND KANSAS CITY
TOLEDO AND ST. LOUIS

Leave Chicago 9:30 P. M.   Leave St. Louis 8:00 P. M.
Leave Chicago 12:30 NOON.   Leave Kansas City 6:30 P. M.
Leave Toledo 2:30 P. M.   Leave St. Louis 6:10 P. M.

Chicago, Detroit & Niagara Falls Short Line.
CHICAGO AND DETROIT

Leave Chicago 8:45 P. M.   Leave Detroit 9:30 P. M.

New York & Boston Express Line, (Via Springfield.) N. Y. N. H. & H. & B & A Rds.
NEW YORK AND BOSTON.

Leave New York 10:30 P. M.   Leave Boston 10:30 P. M.

__PRIVATE CARS.__—The private cars, "Adelina Patti," "Etelka Gerster," and "Janauschek," undoubtedly the handsomest cars in the world, are for hire for short or long trips.

MANN'S BOUDOIR CAR CO. is now prepared to treat with R. R. companies for placing their cars in regular service on their lines. For further particulars and descriptive books apply to

MANN'S BOUDOIR CAR CO.

18 Broadway.   (Welles Building.)   New York.

George Westinghouse, Jr., President 　　H. H. Westinghouse, General Agent.
John Caldwell, Treasurer.　T. W. Welch, Superintendent.　W. W. Card, Secretary.

The Westinghouse ✳ Air-Brake ✳ Co.

PITTSBURGH, PA., U. S. A.

— MANUFACTURERS OF THE —

Westinghouse Automatic Brake,

Westinghouse Locomotive Driver Brake,

Vacuum Brakes,

(Westinghouse and Smith Patents).

✽ WESTINGHOUSE · FREIGHT · BRAKE ✽

THE AUTOMATIC FREIGHT BRAKE is essentially the same apparatus as the Automatic Brake for passenger cars, except that the various parts are so combined as to form practically one piece of mechanism, and is sold at a very low price. The saving in accidents, flat wheels, brakemen's wages, and the increased speed possible with perfect safety, will repay the cost of its application within a very short time.

THE "Automatic" has proved itself to be the most efficient Train and Safety Brake known. Its application is instantaneous; it can be operated from any car in the train if desired, and should the train separate, or hose or pipe fail, it applies automatically. A GUARANTEE is given customers against loss from PATENT SUITS on the apparatus sold them.

The WESTINGHOUSE BRAKE is now fitted to upwards of

12,000 ENGINES AND 60,000 CARS,

and is adopted by the principal Railways in all parts of the world.

Full Information Furnished on Application.

DAILY CAPACITY.

MILL "A," 7,000; MILL "B," 2,000; "ANCHOR," 1500; TOTAL, 10,500 bbls.

Chas. A. Pillsbury & Co.

MERCHANT MILLERS, Minneapolis, Minn.

OUR BRANDS

PILLSBURY'S BEST.		CARLETON.	
DIAMOND.	REFORM.	SUCCESS.	ANCHOR.
MINNESOTA BELLE.		PILLSBURY.	
STRAIGHT.	ALASKA.	CROWN.	TONKA.

These mills are three in number, with a capacity of 10,500 bbls. per day, or nearly 3,000,000 bbls. per year. To feed these mills requires 15,000,000 bushels of wheat annually. Our PILLSBURY A mill has the largest capacity of any mill in the world, consuming over 32,000 bushels of wheat per day. It is supplied with the best machinery known to the milling trade; no expense has been spared to ensure perfection in all details, and it is the most perfect and costly mill on the globe.

In ordering flour, be sure and call for "PILLSBURY'S BEST," as interested parties will try and supply you with an inferior flour upon which they can make a larger profit.

Dilworth, Porter & Co.
(LIMITED)

PITTSBURGH, PA.

RAILROAD·AND·BOAT

SPIKES

GEORGE WESTINGHOUSE, Jr., President
ASAPH T. ROWAND, Secretary
ROBERT PITCAIRN, Treasurer

C. H. JACKSON, Vice-Pres. & Gen'l Manager
HENRY SNYDER, General Agent
HARVEY FIELDEN, Contracting Engineer

CHARLES R. JOHNSON, Signal Engineer

THE
UNION SWITCH AND SIGNAL CO.

SOLE MANUFACTURERS OF IMPROVED

Railway Interlocking, Switching and Signaling Appliances,

WITH AUTOMATIC ELECTRIC LOCKING,

Without Which no Interlocking is Safe.

FROGS, CROSSINGS, SWITCHES AND SWITCH STANDS

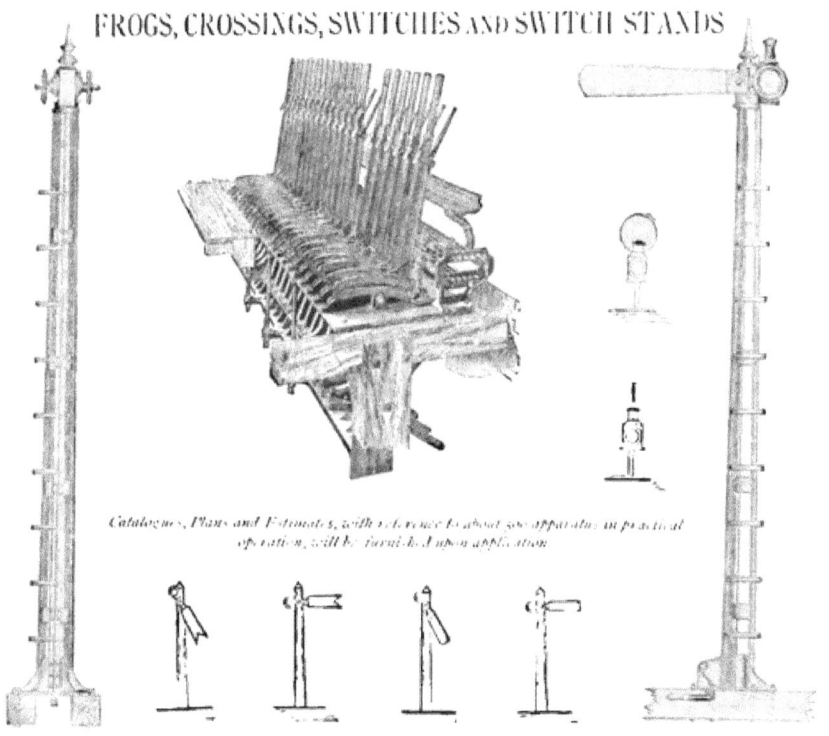

Catalogues, Plans and Estimates, with reference to about 500 apparatus in practical operation, will be furnished upon application.

OFFICE AND WORKS

Corner Garrison Alley and Duquesne Way,
PITTSBURGH, PA., U. S. A.

CARNEGIE BROTHERS & CO.

(LIMITED)

PITTSBURGH, PA.

MANUFACTURERS OF

IRON AND STEEL BEAMS,

CHANNELS, TEES, ANGLES,

STRUCTURAL IRON AND STEEL.

UNUSUAL SIZES AND SHAPES
A SPECIALTY

ESTABLISHED 1783

· TRANSITS, LEVELS, LEVELING RODS, CHAINS, ·

· CHESTERMAN'S TAPES ·

PLANIMETERS, CLYNOMETERS, Etc.

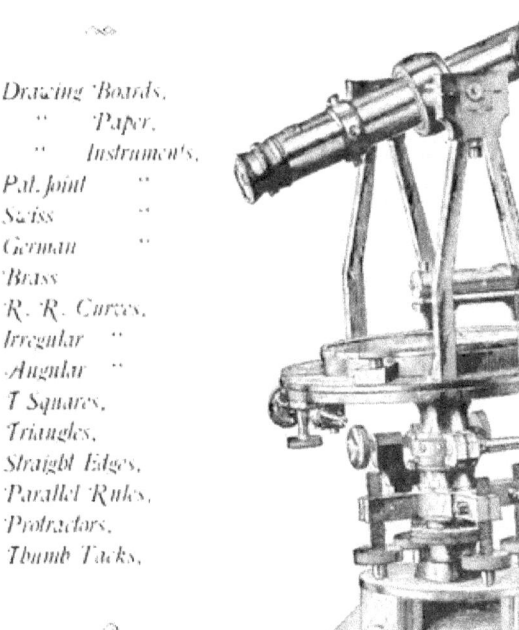

Drawing Boards,
" Paper,
" Instruments,
Pat. Joint "
Swiss "
German "
Brass "
R. R. Curves,
Irregular "
Angular "
T Squares,
Triangles,
Straight Edges,
Parallel Rules,
Protractors,
Thumb Tacks,

India Inks,
Liquid India Inks,
Indelible " "
Indelible Colored Inks
Water Colors,
Moist "
Brushes of all kinds,
Ink Slabs,
Cabinet Saucers,
Whatman's Papers,
Profile "
Cross Section "
Tracing "
Transit Books,
Level "
Field "
Pencils.

CATALOGUES FREE. Send for 5th Edition.

Oswald McAllister,

1226 Chestnut Street,   PHILADELPHIA, PA.

Successor to W. Y. McALLISTER, formerly at 728 Chestnut St.

✻ Pennsylvania Steel Company ✻

SAM'L M. FELTON, President. | L. S. BENT, V. Pres & Gen. Mgr. | At the Works, | S. W. BALDWIN, N. Y. Agt.
 | F. W. WOOD, Superintendent. | STEELTON, PA. | 104 Broadway, New York.

FORGINGS.
of any weight to order.

SHAFTING.
Hammered or Rolled.

Mine and Car Axles

Rail Fastenings.

Spikes, Etc., Etc.

Capacity, 250,000 Tons of Steel per year.

STEEL --- --- RAILS
At Standard **T. RAILS** from 70 lbs. to 16 Patterns of lbs. per Yard.

LIGHT PATTERNS ON STOCK,
with Fastenings, Spikes, etc.

STREET RAILS
AND STEEL CURVES
TO ORDER.

STEEL BLOOMS

SLABS & BILLETS
ROLLED OR HAMMERED

OPEN-HEARTH
or
BESSEMER

Spring and Machinery
· STEEL ·

Interlocking Switching and Signaling Appliances
FOR JUNCTIONS, CROSSINGS, DRAWBRIDGES AND TERMINALS,
Securing Safety from Accidents with Economy of Operation.

STEEL RAIL FROGS. **RAILROAD FROGS AND CROSSINGS,**
Embodying the best Improvements for Durability and Strength.

IMPROVED SWITCHES AND SWITCH STANDS,
Of several different patterns, suited to all uses.

✻ Magneto-Electric-Crossing-Signal ✻

The best in the world for sounding alarm at Highway Crossings, has no battery, requires no winding up, works successfully with attendance at very remote intervals, or moderate cost, and can be set up and put in operation by unskilled persons.

☞ The capacity of the Frog, Switch and Signal Department is very great. Good workmanship and materials always guaranteed, with low prices. For prices or information relating to such work address

GEO. W. PARSONS, Sup't F. S. & S. Department,
STEELTON, PA.

F. W. DEVOE & CO.

ESTABLISHED 1852.

Fulton St., Cor. of William,   NEW YORK.

MANUFACTURERS OF

COACH AND CAR COLORS

GROUND IN JAPAN.

FOR these colors we received the highest award, the Gold Medal, at the National Exposition of Railway Appliances in Chicago.

SPECIAL SHADES MADE TO ORDER.

WE furnish special body colors to Pennsylvania R. R., New York Central, New York & New Haven, Lehigh Valley, New Jersey Central and other large Railroads.

Special Shades for Stations, Freight Cars and Cabooses—Bridge and Roof Paints.

FINE : VARNISHES : AND : JAPANS

FOR COACHES AND CARS.

Wood Fillers, Wood Surfacers, Wood Stains, Hard Oil Finish.

PURE MIXED PAINTS

WE desire to call attention of consumers to the fact that we guarantee our ready-mixed paints to be made only of pure linseed oil and the most permanent pigments. They are not "Chemical," "Rubber," "Patent," or "Fire-proof." We use no secret or patent method in manufacturing them by which benzine and water are made to serve the purpose of pure linseed oil.

SAMPLE CARDS OF 50 DESIRABLE SHADES SENT ON REQUEST.

We manufacture Brushes of every description   **BRUSHES**   for Artists, Painting, Varnishing, Gilding, Striping

WHITE LEAD, ZINC WHITE, COLORS IN OIL.

ARTISTS' MATERIALS

F. W. D. & CO.'S Tube Colors.   F. W. D. & CO.'S Fine Brushes.
F. W. D. & CO.'S Canvas.

OUR Manufactures are used by and command the confidence of the leading artists of the country. A list of those indorsing our goods sent on application.

Crayon, Sculptors' and Etching Materials.   Drawing Papers, Mathematical Instruments.

CORRESPONDENCE INVITED.

COFFIN, DEVOE & CO., 176 Randolph Street, CHICAGO, ILLS.

Ask your Stationer for Esterbrook's Pens

ESTABLISHED 1860. USE THE BEST

ESTERBROOK'S
SUPERIOR
STEEL 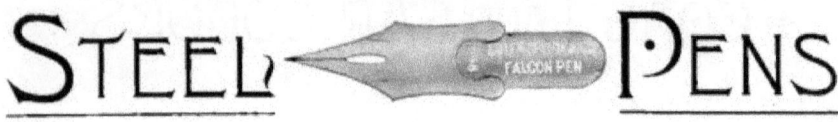 PENS

PENS FOR

All Business Purposes,
    Schools and Colleges,
        Book-Keeping and Correspondence,
            Rapid and Easy Writing.

PENS MADE

In Every Degree of Fineness,
    Of Superior and Standard Quality,
        For Professional and Ornamental Work,
            Of Genuine American Manufacture.

The **Esterbrook Steel Pen Co.** are the manufacturers of the Esterbrook Falcon Pen No. 048, unquestionably the best and most popular business pen in America.

· LEADING STYLES ·

Fine Points, Nos. 232, 333, 444.   Blunt Points, Nos. 122, 183, 1743.
Medium Points, Nos. 14, 130, 048.   Fine Engrossing, Nos. 239, 267, 313.
Elastic Pens, Nos. 120, 128, 135.   Broad Points, Nos. 161, 200, 284.
        Turned up Points, Nos. 256, 301, 1876.

WORKS   **The Esterbrook Steel Pen Co.**   WAREHOUSE
CAMDEN, NEW JERSEY.   26 JOHN ST., NEW YORK.

The Esterbrook Steel Pens have been adopted by the Louisville & Nashville Railroad.

THE EMERSON & FISHER CO.

CARRIAGE BUILDERS

CINCINNATI, O., U.S.A.

CATALOGUE for 1886 — SEND FOR

THE OLDEST, LARGEST AND BEST MANUFACTURERS OF MODERATE-PRICED VEHICLES. ANNUAL CAPACITY: 20,000 CARRIAGES.

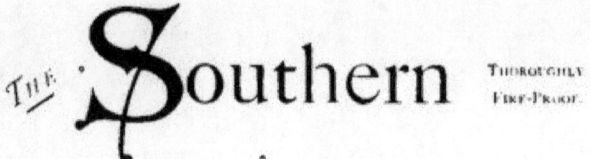

The Southern

Thoroughly Fire-Proof

THE SOUTHERN HOTEL, cor. Fifth and Walnut Sts., St. Louis, Mo., has a frontage on four different streets — its rotunda forming a true cross 330 feet in length, running from North to South, and 330 feet in length from East to West, sixty feet in width and a twenty-foot ceiling.

THE building is six stories high, has five elevators and every other modern convenience, and it is the most thoroughly fire-proof hotel in America. The entire interior construction is of iron, cement and concrete.

THE proprietors so believe in its infallibility, that they do not carry one Dollar of insurance on the building or furniture.

IT is the most convenient and suitable hotel in the city for public and private entertainment, both on account of the completeness of its appointments, and the elegance and taste of the general arrangement.

IT has four hundred rooms, with a sleeping capacity of from eight hundred to one thousand persons. It is a perfect model of order and cleanliness.

THE rates of board are reasonable, from three to five dollars per day. Price fixed from location and space occupied.

SHAKESPEARE

AULT & WIBORG,

𝔏etter 𝔓ress 𝔏ithographic 𝔍nks and 𝔉ine 𝔙arnishes

FOOT OF NEW STREET,

CINCINNATI, OHIO.

No. 28 Rose Street, New York.   BRANCH OFFICES.   178 & 180 Monroe St., Chicago.

Pacific Oil Co.

F. MUKSMAN, Pres. & Tres.
J. L. PARMELEE, V-----
J. L. SKIDMORE, S-

Producers and Manufacturers of

Refined Tallow and Car Grease
· Lubricating Oils ·

RAILWAY LUBRICATING SUPPLIES A SPECIALTY.

PASSENGER CAR GREASE.
KOHINOOR
TRADE MARK
KOHINOOR
FREIGHT CAR GREASE.

SOLE MANUFACTURER
OF
Paris Valve Oil,
Famous Cylinder Oil,
Ruby Engine,
Kohinoor Freight Car Grease,
Kohinoor Coach Grease.

Manufacturers of

· FAMOUS BOILER COMPOUND ·

· FAMOUS STEAM PACKING ·

Branch House:
FT. SCOTT, KAS.

OFFICE, 521 North Second St.
ST. LOUIS, MO.

M. M. Buck & Co.

Manufacturers and Dealers in Every Article used in Constructing and Operating Railroads; Steamboat, Telegraph, Miners', Foundry, Machinists' and Contractors' Supplies.

Frogs, Crossings, Switches, Jacks, Tank Valves, Spikes, Bolts, Head Lights, Car Fixtures, Lamps, Lanterns, Locks, Car Brasses, etc. Ingot Copper and other Metals, Boiler Flues, Belting, Hose, Packing, Tools, Machinery, "Tanite" Emery Wheels and Grinders.

207 and 209 North Third Street.

St. Louis, Mo.

A TRIUMPH OF MODERN CHEMISTRY IS
The · Harden · Star · Hand · Grenade.

THE introduction of the "Hand Grenade" marks an era in the history of Fire Appliances. The costly, cumbersome, and complicated Chemical Extinguishers are giving way to the simpler, cheaper and more powerful Grenade.

Modern experience shows that the most successful way to fight fire in its earlier stages is with chemicals, and it further shows that in the "Hand Grenade" is found the simplest and most practical means of applying them.

1,088 Actual Fires Extinguished with them in 1885, saving Millions of Dollars.

EXTRACTS FROM THE PUBLIC PRESS.

"A simple and powerful extinguisher on the premises, ready for instant use, is better than a fire department several blocks away."

"THE first five minutes at a fire is better than the next half hour."

"THE Grenade may not be infallible, but it seems nearer so than any other appliance."

"HE who fails to provide his home with Hand Grenades is shouldering a fearful responsibility."

"THE record of the HARDEN Star Grenade is unparalleled in the history of fire appliances."

"THE extinguishment by the Hand Grenade of a thousand actual fires, and scores of them, when used by women and children, saving millions of dollars worth of property, and all within twenty months, is a marvelous record."

"IT costs less to protect property with the Hand Grenades than with any other appliance, and the protection is the best that can be had."

Adopted by Thirteen Railway Companies, for use in Depots, Shops, etc.

AMONG THEM ARE

THE OREGON RAILWAY & NAVIGATION COMPANY,
THE SOUTHERN PACIFIC RAILROAD,
THE UNION PACIFIC RAILWAY,
THE CINCINNATI, HAMILTON & DAYTON R. R.,
THE CHICAGO & GRAND TRUNK RAILROAD,
THE MICHIGAN CENTRAL RAILROAD,
THE C. C. C. & I. RAILWAY,
THE K. C., FT. SCOTT & GULF RAILROAD,
THE D. & R. G. & W. RAILWAY.

The Purchases of above Roads aggregate 78,720 Grenades.

The Grenades are now made in two Sizes—Pints and Quarts.

☞ SEND FOR DESCRIPTIVE CIRCULAR.

HARDEN · HAND · GRENADE · FIRE · EXTINGUISHER · CO.
51 & 53 Dearborn Street,
CHICAGO, ILLS.

R. P. PATTISON, PRESIDENT
H. H. CROSS, GEN'L MANAGER
C. H. ALLEN, SECRETARY.

www.ingramcontent.com/pod-product-compliance
Lightning Source LLC
Chambersburg PA
CBHW031121160426
43192CB00008B/1070